naked play

Katchadorian

And God Loves Each One (homosexuality)

So That's How I Was Born

Sex Education Dictionary for
Today's Teens & Pre Teens Dr. Dean
Hoch

It's Okay To Say No Robin Lenett

The New You Richard Bimler

What To Say after you clear your throat

A PARENTS' GUIDE
TO SEX EDUCATION

Jean S. Gochos

PRESS PACIFICA 1980

Library of Congress Cataloging in Publication Data

Gochros, Jean S.
    What to say after you clear your throat.

    Bibliography: p. 224
    Includes index.
    1. Sex instruction.   I. Title.
HQ57.G63   301.41'07   79-16042
ISBN 0-916630-18-8

Cover design by Jane Wilkins Pultz.

Manufactured in the United States of America.
Press Pacifica, P.O. Box 1227, Kailua Hawaii, 96734.

This book is dedicated to Harvey, Susan and David
and
to all adults, who know just exactly what to say about sex
until it's time to say it.

TABLE OF CONTENTS

ACKNOWLEDGMENTS

As a child, I often wondered why anyone wrote acknowledgments, and who on earth read them. Now I understand why they are written, for a book (at least this one) is not only the author's work, but rather the sum total of the thinking, love and work of many people. I certainly hope that those who so well deserve the following words of thanks read them.

My good friend Connie Lister (and I suspect Larry, too) has given unstinting help from the first draft—complete with single spacing, chicken scratches and muddy canine footprints—through the finished product. Without her ability to help me organize my thoughts as well as my words, this book would never have gotten off the ground, or rather, the dining room table.

Catherine Harris of the Honolulu Writer's Association read the entire book at breakneck speed, wielding an efficient editorial pencil that managed to weed out the many unnecessary redundancies that neither Connie nor I had caught.

Dr. Vince Defeo of the University of Hawaii took time out from his busy schedule to act as consultant on physiology, and I am indebted to him for his help.

My thanks also go to Raul and Mary Nell Leyba and to Katherine Woodard, who provided not only time, but objectivity when my own had waned.

I am indeed grateful to Natalie Mondschein and Winifred Kempton for providing consultation in the area of retardation.

Many people were indirectly helpful. Whether they were children or adults, students, friends or colleagues, they contributed thinking, questions, concerns, and personal vignettes. My uncle, Bernard Schaar, first brought the term "serendipity" to my attention. He has made his own valuable contributions to the study of its use, and I wish he could know how much impact he had on me. My parents, Marian and Clarence Schaar, despite any shortcomings noted in this book, were far more honest and helpful about sex than many, if not most parents of their generation. They at least tried where others failed, and most of the values I have tried to give to my own children are derived from them.

Most of all I must thank my own family. Many spouses and children have earned the gratitude of authors for putting up with the haphazard living conditions under which books are written. Mine, too, have borne the strain with remarkable good grace. But even more, they have provided real help. My husband, Harvey, has shared with me his time, his advice, and his bookshelf, and his own work in the area of human sexuality has formed the basis of much of my own thinking. My children, David and Susan, have courageously let me use them as illustrative examples and have shared their own thinking with me, with candor and maturity that went far beyond the call of duty. Even Grendel, the new four-footed member of our family, has helped out by keeping me company as I typed, without walking on any of the final drafts.

To all of you, then, for your considerable time, patience and help, my very fond

Mahalo and Aloha.

Jean Gochros
Honolulu

CHAPTER 1

WHAT? ANOTHER BOOK ON SEX EDUCATION?

What to say after you clear your throat is a book about the *art* of communicating with youth between the ages of one and twenty one, and also some adults, about sex. It is written for people who consider themselves reasonably intelligent and well informed, yet who still find themselves confused about how to give the helpful sex education that they want to provide.

If you are one of those people, know that you are not alone. In workshops, courses and lectures I give to parents and to professionals such as teachers, doctors, psychologists and social workers, I am continually impressed by two things: the anxiety and fear people still have about sex education, and the hunger to know more about *how* to give it.

I am besieged by questions asking for definitive answers. Should we give sex education or shouldn't we? At what age should it start? Who should receive it? Who should give it? Should it be formal or informal? Where should it be given? Should books and pictures be allowed? Should we give biology, hygiene or morality? And if morality, whose morality? Yours? Mine? And finally, "What should we do *if.* . . ?" "What do you say *when.* . . ?"

No matter how many books they may have read on sex or sex education, many people still find it difficult to translate general knowledge and values into everyday conversations and relationships. They are at a loss when confronted by situations that do not fit or are not covered by the books they've read; often they are convinced that there is only one right answer, and that if they do not find it, they will have failed as parents or professionals.

Sex education, however, involves interpersonal relationships, which in turn involve complicated communication skills. This is where art comes in, and is an area that has been sadly neglected. Too often people receive the impression that sex education requires merely a basic core of knowledge, a few guidelines to the questions children tend to ask, with cut and dried answers to those questions. Often the only attention paid to the art and skills of communication are implied or even stated rules, like "always be comfortable, relaxed and warm," "never answer before you are asked or more than you are asked," and "always be honest."

These are good, sensible rules, and few people disagree with them. But putting them into practice can be another matter, because they are based on certain assumptions that don't always apply. Some examples are as follows:

Myth—Children will always ask or tell you what's on their minds.

Children are often refreshingly less inhibited than adults. But they don't always tell you what's on their minds. Why should they? Do you? How often do you communicate to your spouse, friend, or lover a question or thought on an important, sensitive subject like sex the minute you think of it? At best, it's probably only part of the time. Usually it just doesn't seem like the right moment, or you can't think how to put it into words, or the phone rings, and by the time the right time comes, you've forgotten all about it. That can happen several times before you get around to it, and sometimes a whole marriage goes by without people sharing some of those thoughts. Communication, by the way, is one of the biggest problems people have about sex, and many of the exercises given in this book will help adults as well as children. Thus if you always wait for children to ask, they can become adults with children of their own before you find out what they were thinking and wondering about sex.

Myth—Children will ask questions in a definite order at specific ages.

Although there may be some general sequence of questions that they will ask, many parents will expect at four, "Where did I come from?" at five, "How did I get out?" and at six, "How did I get in?" Unfortunately the children have not read the rule books and may ask the most complex questions first, or may not ask any questions at all.

Myth—You will always be around when they think of a question.

Obviously, you won't. Sometimes you will be at work, or at the store. They may wait until you get home, or if there is someone else around, they may ask that person. If they get an answer that satisfies them, they may never ask you the question.

Myth—You will always have the answer.

That's impossible. Even if you were Masters and Johnson you wouldn't have all the answers. Sometimes you forget them—especially with questions that fluster you. Sometimes it isn't even important to know them all. And sometimes there just are no conclusive answers.

Myth—Complete honesty is both possible and always good.

Of course one should be honest. Who will argue with that? But honest about what? How much detail is necessary for honesty? There are times when complete honesty may frighten or confuse, not help. What do you do then?

Myth—Sex education, if you know the rules, is perfectly simple.

This and the two assumptions that follow make me angry, because I have seen them bring so much grief to people. While sex education could be a lot easier, and I hope that it will be after you read this book, it is not always simple. Children ask questions which the books have never thought of. We are faced with questions and issues today which were not problems in our parents' youth. Anyone who thinks all answers are easy is apt to be thinking in such simplistic terms that he or she can hardly be helpful to a child living in a world where there is such a confusing array of answers.

Myth—Anyone who questions sex education programs in school is uptight and neurotic.

Sex education programs in school are not always adequate or helpful; parents, no matter why they are concerned about such programs, are rightly concerned about who is giving the education and what is being taught. Excessive fear about such programs often stems mainly from misconceptions about what sex education means.

Myth—There is a right way and a wrong way to give sex education, and if you choose the wrong way, you will turn children into sex maniacs or cause them to be inhibited and repressed.

The right way versus the wrong way approach to sex education unfortunately often stems from professionals, such as the psychologist, the doctor, or the social worker. The professionals never intended to create such impressions, but when they speak, we accord them so much authority, we assume that theirs is the right way without questioning it.

The result of all these assumptions is that people tiptoe their way through sex education, scared half-to-death of doing the wrong thing, or of appearing foolish and uptight. Some people are so afraid that they try their best to do nothing. This is unfortunate because despite all the complexities and frustrations, sex education is probably less difficult than most of the things that adults teach children every day of their lives. And it can be much more. fun.

Although the table of contents has given you a general idea of what you will find in this book, a few comments are in order here. It is not the only book you will want to read. Any book is limited by the author's particular areas of expertise and interest, and by space limitations. While there will be necessary overlapping, this book will try to supplement, not repeat other books, emphasizing the art of integrating knowledge, values, and communication skills. Hence examples found in a special section on teachers or handicapped children will also be useful to parents, other professionals, or parents of other children.

No sex expert has all the answers, nor do I, and the suggestions I do have are not necessarily right. They are only guidelines for you to use or to discard as you see fit. There are no cookbooks with never-fail recipes in this area.

I do write on the assumption that most people want children to receive responsible sex education, and that the only disagreements may come with where, how, and by whom it should be given, or with what should be included. Often a situation might be handled in many ways, depending upon the intent at a given moment or on one's values. It is the aim of this book to provide exercises and information to help you deal with differences and decision making, to decrease fear and enhance communication, and generally, to put some fun into talking with people of all ages about sex.

CHAPTER TWO

MYTHS AND REALITIES ABOUT SEX EDUCATION

A logical question at this point would be, "What is sex education?" Unfortunately, it is a difficult question to answer because there are many myths and misconceptions about it that upset parents and block any attempt on their part to deal with the subject. So let's talk about those myths before we attempt to define it.

They fall into two categories: 1. Myths about how people learn and how they behave. 2. Myths about sex education itself.

Myths About Learning and Behavior

There are, for our purposes, two misconceptions about how people learn and behave:

Myth Number One: Learning is almost always verbal, teachers are only teaching when they're talking, and learners are mainly learning in some kind of verbal exchange of ideas.

While we often seem to act on that assumption, we know that isn't true. Watch infants as they discover their hands or toes, teach themselves to roll over, or grab for something just beyond their reach. One can almost see and hear the wheels turning in their minds with each motion. They can't utter a word, they know no words to think with, and we don't really know how they think. Yet, they are obviously learning.

True, words help. But the need to talk, talk, talk is not always shared by all people or cultures, no matter how smart they may be. People learn whether they are young or old, and do not learn just from being talked to or lectured. Their learning may take the shape of listening, thinking and observing. Sometimes the best learning takes place by osmosis without a person even being conscious of it, as any good advertiser knows.

Why do we stress this aspect of learning? Because one of the misconceptions is that sex education is only being given when one is lecturing, that only verbal people can profit by it, and that unless people are asking questions, they are not interested in or curious about sexual matters. People who operate according to this myth will probably not try to give information to children under three, or maybe even under twelve, because such children may not talk as much about sex. They will not think retarded children are interested or capable of learning because many such children—especially "trainables"—do not easily communicate verbally.

A good portion of sex education, however, is non-verbal, and much of what people learn about sex is not from what is said, but from what is *not* said. It is learned from what is seen, felt, or read. When people learn from hearing, it is often not from what others are saying *to* them, but what others are saying *around* them. It is also learning other sounds connected with what they are already seeing or hearing, or inflections which give special interpretations to the spoken words.

One sex educator states that the best sex education children can have is to see their father patting their mother on the rump, and to note that she enjoys it. Children can learn something about sex by exploring themselves. They learn without words that penises or vaginas feel good to touch. Nobody tells them that, and they do not need to be very intelligent to find it out by themselves.

Children who wander into a bedroom when their parents are undressed learn something about adult bodies all by themselves. If the parents rush to hide themselves, the children learn something else. It may be an attitude, perhaps, but that attitude is a fact, and the children absorb it. If the parents stand and chat, the children learn a different attitude. If they walk by a theater with a picture of a naked girl on the billboard, they get one piece of information. If people come out smiling, they get another. If their mother rushes them past, strolls by without reacting, or pauses to look at the billboard herself, they learn something from whatever behavior she exhibits. They learn from whether the "Playboys" are placed on the highest book shelf in the house or

strewn casually on the coffee table. They get some information if
parents discuss pregnancy or some sexually related topic in the living room; they get other information if parents discuss such matters behind closed doors. They learn from muffled sounds in the
bedroom, from tones of voices, frowns, laughs, snickers and whispers that accompany talk of sex, and from the hush that falls
when they suddenly walk in on a conversation. Most of these
above illustrations, even when words are heard are not direct verbal communications to the child, and sometimes non-verbal
sounds outweigh the verbal ones. A father may tell a child that sex
is perfectly natural and nothing to be ashamed of, but if his voice
is ten degrees lower and his face is sober and stern, that fact
teaches the child more than any of the spoken words.

Myth Number Two: People will not think a thought until it
is suggested, and as soon as they think about it, they will act on
that thought.

How many parents and teachers must wish that education
could be that easily controlled. If it were, they could get Johnny
to clean his room the minute they suggested it, and Janie would
devote a lot more time to homework. True, sometimes people can
guide another's thinking and introduce new ideas. Occasionally
someone will jump on a new idea and act impulsively. Usually,
however, that happens only because the person has touched on an
idea the child has been thinking about for a long time.

Yet many people fear that if they talk to a child about sexual
behavior—say, intercourse—they will be "planting" an idea in the
child's head. They fear the child will suddenly develop a new interest and will then run right out and attempt intercourse with
someone.

I suppose there are exceptions but for the most part if a child
has really never thought about intercourse before, it takes a lot
more than talking about it to develop an "interest." In fact,
children's, including some teenagers' first reaction to the whole
idea, is often an emphatic "yuk." If they seem interested, it is
probably because they have been for some time. Even then, they
will have to mull it over in their minds for a long time before
doing anything about it. Early fantasies about sex are usually
because children and teenagers are a bit scared about it all, and
handle their feelings through fantasy.

And how about you? Haven't you ever had an unacceptable

thought? Perhaps it was about "telling off" your boss or one of your in-laws, or indulging in some "improper" sexual behavior. How many times have you acted on such fantasies? If they had real potential for hurting yourself or someone else, probably never.

In fact, fantasies are interesting phenomena. They can be a rehearsal for acceptable behavior so that people can plan how to function effectively; but they can act as safety valves for unacceptable impulses by providing an acceptable outlet. For example, people can relieve tension by shouting at their employer in fantasy, and then have less need to shout in the real situation, when tact might be all important.

In sex, a person "rehearses" acceptable behavior for years, starting with childhood's "playing house" and continuing with fantasies about intercourse during adolescence. Also a person who relieves tension via an orgasm during a fantasy, has less need to act on an unacceptable sexual impulse.

These examples are not meant to suggest that people never go on to experiment, nor that you can prevent a person from having intercourse just by encouraging fantasies. In fact, we would worry about people who spend so much time rehearsing acceptable behavior that they never go out to meet the real world. It's just that you needn't fear that planned sex education will lead children astray. Thoughts are not actions and do not hurt anyone. Where you think your comments might be misunderstood you can qualify them in such a way as to reduce the possibility of their leading to impulsive action.

You can be honest about sex without worrying that you will plant unacceptable ideas in innocent minds or seduce people into unacceptable behavior.

Myths About Sex Education

Myth Number One: **Sex education is a course like biology.**

This myth implies that sex education is a course like biology, that starts at an appointed hour, at an appointed place, gives a set number of facts, and lasts a designated number of minutes. It therefore assumes that adults can completely control time and place, content, what is learned, and who will be the instructor and the recipient.

People who believe this myth are the ones who ask, "Should we give sex education or shouldn't we?" "At what age should we start?" and "Should we give it at home or at school?"

As you have already begun to see, sex education comes from many sources, in many ways, and at many stages of life. It is a "process" more than a "course" that begins at the first moment of life and keeps going until the day we die. This may be easier to understand later when we discuss some ideas about what "sex" is, for it encompasses emotions and attitudes about love, warmth, intimacy, physical sensations that may have nothing whatsoever to do with intercourse and a sense of who one is and what kind of person he or she is.

Sex education, then, begins the first time babies are handled. For the first year, life is mostly composed of "sensual" feelings, such as the pleasure of sucking from the bottle or breast, the way in which the mothers handle the babies' genitals (matter of factly or gingerly), the sense of warmth and security when their mothers hold them close. Infants don't think about these things, of course, they just get messages that become a part of them.

If you tell a child who is masturbating to "Take your hand out of your pocket," that's sex education. If you say, "Don't do that, that's naughty," that's sex education. And if you don't do or say anything, that's sex education too.

You can deliberately plan to never give any sex education, but you will be kidding yourself. Your children will get sex education in your home and you will give it to them. You can refuse to allow children to participate in a school program, but they will still get sex education in school. They will get information from other children. Being left out is sex education. They will get it in the way the bathrooms are set up, in the talk around the playground and in what they are not taught. Children learn about how all the other organs work; when facts about sexual organs are the only things not taught, that in itself tells them something.

As a teacher, you can plan never to say anything at all about sex, and stick to it. But the children will still get sex education in your class, and you will probably give it to them. You will give it when you either react or don't react to words or comments, when you choose words to designate going to the bathroom and when you pass over a question.

Doctors will give sex education in the way they handle an examination, in the way they talk, or don't talk, about sexual matters. Ministers also will give sex education in the way they discuss sin and love.

Children, then, are going to get sex education, not "one way or another", as we often say, but in all ways. They will get it in the streets, over the radio, through television and in the newspapers, in the school, from their friends, from your neighbors— everywhere. *You have no choice about it!*

What's more, we keep on getting sex education even as older adults. When our children say to us, "Gee, you don't think about sex anymore," or "You're too old to have a baby," or "Look at that dirty old man," we are getting sex education. When a couple married for fifty years goes to a nursing home and gets put into separate bedrooms, that's sex education. So you can see, it goes on and on. Sex education is all around us. It can't be avoided.

Much of that education, of course, is unplanned. It may or may not agree with what we had planned to give, or with our own values about sex. It may or may not be what someone had meant to give. All that is strictly chance.

The only decision to be made about sex education is who is going to give what to any person at a particular moment, by plan. The only choice we have is how much planned education we ourselves will either try to give or encourage.

Myth Number two: Sex education is always formal.

As you have seen, it isn't. It can be a formal, semester-long course three times a week, a formal "quickie" session every day for one week, an occasional informal "rap" session, a two-minute response to a quick question, a one-minute comment, a palnned "non-response" to an action or word, a look or a snicker.

Myth Number Three: There is a right way and a wrong way to give it.

The introduction to this book has already questioned this myth. There are many "rights", and who's to say what's a "wrong" way? These terms are frightening and not particularly useful. It is far more important to think through what will be "helpful" to a child rather than to worry about someone else's definition of right and wrong.

Myth Number Four: **All you need to teach is biology.**
Only a small part of sex is biology, and even most of that is not necessary to know. The trouble with most sex education "courses" is that they leave out the important information, which has less to do with anatomy than it has to do with people and how they get along with each other.

There have been studies made which found that mere knowledge about biology and contraception plays a relatively minor role in determining future sexual behavior. For example, in one study of college students, while ninety percent of the girls had been given information about menstruation, seventy percent about where babies come from, and thirty percent about sexual intercourse, there was significantly less promiscuity* in the girls who had received both facts and values about a wide range of topics, including orgasm, the pleasures of sex, venereal disease, masturbation, and the difficulty of controlling sexual feelings.

Myth Number Five A and B: Although the two myths are contradictory, they are often held at the same time by the same people. Myth Five A is that **nobody should teach sex but a sex expert**, who needs to know all the thousand and one things that there are about sex. Myth Five B holds that **anyone can give sex education.** Sex is such a natural instinct that no special knowledge is needed for either the teacher or the learner.

Neither extreme is correct. Much of sex takes place not in the genitals but in the head, and people do need information to be able to use their instincts effectively and wisely. We are human beings with emotions, and with social consequences for our behavior. You do need to have some basic information about biology and human sexual behavior. You do not, however, need to be a doctor or a Masters or Johnson to be a helpful sex educator. You do not need to have all the facts at your immediate disposal. You merely need to be aware of what you do not know, have the courage to admit it and the ability and willingness to help the child get additional information.

This myth includes the notion that if adults do not always know the right answer they will look foolish to the child. Chil-

---

*   While the word "promiscuity" was used in the study, and defined in a specific way, I'm sure the authors would agree that such a term is nebulous, based on personal value judgments.

dren are not usually that demanding. Mostly, youngsters require honesty and a willingness to help. People who expect much more of themselves and try to bluff their way through are doing more harm and making it harder on themselves, than if they had said, "I don't know—let's find out."

Myth Number Six: The adult is totally responsible for what the child learns.

You know that old adage about leading a horse to water? Well, it applies here. Your responsibility is to make it possible for children to learn by giving them access to correct information and new ideas. Beyond that, it is their job. Besides, it is impossible to control what children learn. They are learning from many different sources, at different rates, at different times. People who place all the blame on themselves if children do not learn what they have tried to teach, are doing themselves a disservice. It is no wonder that the thought of sex education scares them.

Myth Number Seven: All sex educators should agree.

That myth is both naive and impossible. Some "sex educators" are the kids in the streets, and you sure wouldn't always want to agree with them. Even experts disagree. True, we hope for some consistency so that the child won't get caught in a battle between parent and teacher, or parent versus parent and become completely confused.

Human beings hold a wide variety of perspectives which sometimes means disagreements; children should be helped to understand this as early as possible. What's more important is how we handle disagreements.

Myth Number Eight: Sex education is a serious business.

Sex and sex education are important. But that doesn't mean that everything important has to be deadly serious. Just as there is humor in other important areas of life, so there is humor in sex. The more important the topic, the more people use—and need—a bit of humor to help them cope with it. We use humor about marriage, money, sickness—even death. Yet many people are afraid to deal with sex in a lighthearted, casual manner. Interestingly enough, people who think of sex as deadly serious and treat all humor about it as if it were obscene, often snicker the loudest at dirty jokes, or at the mere mention of the word "sex." The deadly serious approach to sex education surrounds it with mystique that gives it an importance out of proportion to its place in every day living. It is more important to distinguish between a casual, humorous attitude toward sex, and a snickering, flip attitude toward it.

By way of summary, let's pull together all those myths and their answers and let's define sex education as the giving of facts and attitudes about human sexuality and human sexual behavior. Sex education takes place continually, everywhere. It is both verbal and non-verbal, formal and informal, planned and unplanned. We have no choice about sex education that is unplanned; it happens, and by chance, it may or may not agree with what we have planned. Planned sex education requires a little knowledge about general human behavior, biology, the ability to discern between fact and opinion and the honesty to admit which it is, plus the willingness to recognize gaps in your own knowledge and to help the child use other appropriate sources.

Remember that I am defining such terms as "teenager" or "child" very broadly, often ignoring the usual age classifications. At any given time, the "child" I discuss might be four, fourteen, twenty-four, forty-eight, eighty-four years old, or potentially all of the above. It will be important for you to do two things. 1. Remind yourself that the basic principles of effective sex education hold true for all ages. 2. Play around with any subject or example. See if it might apply to different age categories, and how it might have to be modified to fit the needs of both the general age group and the individual person in whom you are interested.

CHAPTER THREE

PLANNED SEX EDUCATION

The most helpful sex education is planned education or at least maximizes the amount of planned education and minimizes the amount of unplanned education.

Does "planned" mean "formal rigid blueprint" or that everything said is carefully thought out and prepared? NO! "Planned" only means that:

1. It is based on your definite decision that you want a child provided with useful sex education and that you want input into that education. How much input you will want may depend on your role.

2. It is based on some advance thought about what kind of information you want that child to eventually have, and what kind of attitudes and values you wish him or her to have.

3. It is based on some advance thought and planning, or "anticipation" and "rehearsal" about how you will provide that information and those values.

While planning can sometimes be long range, formal and exact, it can often be short term and casual. The best kind of planning, for example, starts before a baby is born, but if your child is already seventeen, you can still plan what you want to give from now on. You can even plan some education for your 60 year old mother. That "plan" may consist merely of thinking over some new ideas expressed on a recent TV show and intending to share your opinions with your mother. Remember, too, that the "education," when it occurs, may be as casual as a one-line remark, based on your thinking. Of course you cannot plan what education your mother or any other person will actually receive, you can only plan what you will try to give. Further, any long range plan will need periodic revision and great flexibility, because you neither know what the future holds nor how your thinking may change.

Let's explore those three points at more length.

First is your decision that you want a person to have helpful sex education, and that you want to have some input into that education.

If you are a parent, you will probably decide that you want as much input as you can possibly achieve. You may also, however, need to make decisions not only about your own children, but about your children's friends, children of your own friends, neighbors, nieces or nephews, or parents. That is not because you consider it your job—or even your right—to educate them, but because it is possible that you will be doing it anyhow, to some degree, in an unplanned way.

Second, you probably have some strong opinions about sex and what sort of information children need to have by the time they become adults. You may not have really thought through your ideas and sometimes your emotional reactions may contradict what your head is thinking. What are your opinions about masturbation (self-stimulation), kissing, petting, pre-marital sex, birth control, abortion, or the sexual revolution? How did you feel about sex as a teenager? What information about intercourse, or oral sex for instance, might have been helpful to you in your adult relationships? How do you feel about yourself and your role as a man or woman, husband or wife, and parent? How do you feel about rape? What worries do you have about your children? What values do you consider important in sexual—or all other—personal relationships? And what attitudes do you have that you don't like and that you want to avoid passing on to your children? Believe it or not, these are only a few of the things to consider. If you do not know yourself and your own attitudes, you will find it much more difficult to transmit your values to others.

You can't avoid giving some "unplanned" attitudes, because in real situations, you act spontaneously, and that is as it should be. If you have sifted through some of your ideas ahead of time, you will greatly increase the chances of having your "unplanned" education be consistent with your well-thought-out ideas. Also, in order to overcome attitudes you dislike in yourself, it helps to know what they are and how you got them. Then if you can't avoid passing on your attitudes to your children, at least you can be honest about them and give your children a better perspective.

You might find that like many people you may hold conflicting values. As you sort through your feelings you may find yourself more confused than you realized, but if you are, it's important to know about it ahead of time. People usually, however, find that their basic values are fairly easy to state.

I want my son and daughter to know that sex is more than just intercourse, that it involves a wide range of emotions and expressions. It can be a sense of one's self-worth as a man or woman, a merely physical enjoyment of one's own body, a complex human relationship, a complete act of intercourse, oral sex, or an affectionate gesture.

I want them to know that whatever form it takes, it is an important part of life that can produce great joy or great misery. They should understand that people share responsibility for the consequences of any action they take affecting themselves or others (including unborn babies).

I want them to know that while sex is often an expression of love, the two words are not synonymous and love does not automatically produce a good physical relationship. I want them to realize that while the best sex includes a sense of warmth, intimacy, and affection, any sexual relationship should be based on dignity, self respect, concern for others, and respect for others' values and wishes. Finally, I want my children to know that while I do not have answers for all the problems they may face, I will always be ready to try to help them.

This is not a complete list by any means, and you may agree or disagree with all or any part of it. That's for you to decide.

Supposing you agree with all of my ideas. They are only words, ideas, a philosophy. Translating such a philosophy into everyday situations is another matter. How do you do it? If you give a lecture, children will be bored in five minutes, and even if they aren't, you'll have just transferred words and ideas from your head to theirs. To begin with, most of us have trouble putting such thoughts into words, primarily because we don't want to sound maudlin, and we haven't had much experience.

Here is some homework that can help you at least put your ideas into words.

Sit down with your husband, wife, or friend, and talk about what values you consider important. Take one of the questions I raised and discuss it. Be as honest as possible about your doubts, worries, confusions, and feelings of embarrassment. Try using words like "penis" and "vagina" or even their slang equivalents, and see how you feel about them. Discuss your feelings. You might talk with your sexual partner about the things you like and dislike in your own sexual relationships. Emphasize the things you like, though, for if you put too much emphasis on the negatives, you will both come away from the discussion feeling very unhappy. Above all try to be honest; and don't be surprised if you discover that that's hard to do because you have never really sat down and talked this way before.

Bonus assignment:

Unless you are discussing details of your own sexual relationships, carry on this discussion when your children are around—perhaps at the dinner table or in the living room. If they are old enough to carry on a reasonably intelligent conversation, you might try to include them in the discussion; what do they think kids want to know, how do they feel about people who are different from them in any way (e.g. fat, skinny, a different color— it needn't be limited to sexual differences)? What do they think is important in a friendship, family, or marriage? You may not get an answer, but it makes no difference; it is a "door opener."

Third   there is the usefulness of anticipation and rehearsal. Many questions you get will not call for discussing attitudes, and when children ask questions on the spur of the moment, there is no time to sit and think about it and mull it over in your mind. You have to answer quickly and that is where so much "unplanned" education comes in. The answer that you give and the way in which you give it will be largely emotional; it may or may not be the answer you would give if you had time to stop and think for thirty minutes. But if you can anticipate ahead of time what questions or problems might come up, and rehearse by thinking about and carrying on conversations in fantasy about how you might deal with them, you will greatly increase the chances of answering the way you really want to.

Of course you'll never be able to anticipate everything, and you'll probably goof at times. It's just a question of having the odds in your favor instead of against you.

What are the questions or comments that you may have to deal with?

First there are the usual questions to be found in most other books on reproduction and I won't spend too much time on them. Mostly they are: "Where do babies come from?" (or "Where did I come from?") "How does the baby get out?" "How does the baby get in?" "How does the father plant a seed?"

Sometimes you can take each question as it comes, with a thinking space between, but sometimes you may need to combine answers quickly. For example:

"Babies come from a special spot inside the mother, about here (and you point to it) called the uterus. They grow from a tiny egg inside the mother. The father put his penis inside the mother's vagina and a kind of thick liquid called semen came out. The semen held some special tiny seeds called sperm. A sperm and the mother's egg joined together and grew into a baby. The mother's uterus made a nice soft room where the baby could keep on growing and when it was ready, it came out just the way it got in— through the vagina."

The separate questions usually start at around three or four years of age—sometimes earlier, sometimes later. The longer story becomes useful as the child gets closer to five years of age, and is easiest to give if he already knows the terms "penis" and "vagina." If he doesn't you'll have to explain.

Some tips:

You might avoid the usual "Mommy's tummy" explanation of where the baby comes from, because some children think that that means babies are a result of eating, or that the baby can get lost in the digestive tract. If you forget, don't worry about it, but be on the alert for such an idea, or correct yourself some other time.

Try to avoid the concept "planting a seed," or if you use it, try to explain it a little more concretely. You'd be surprised at how many children visualize flowers growing inside the mother's stomach.

Often books sound as if such questions are stated just that way. But when my child was about three, her first question while she was getting dressed was, "Will you buy me a baby?" The rest of the conversation went something like this: "You don't buy babies, they grow in mothers' stomachs." (I goofed in using the word "stomach," but my daughter grew up okay anyhow.)

"Would you grow me one?"

"Maybe, some time."

"Goodie! Do it right now! How do you do it?"

"Well, I can't do it right now. Mothers and fathers together start babies growing. A mother can't do it all by herself."

Once she found that mothers needed help, my daughter wasn't interested in staying around to find out how they start, and rushed off to play with her friends. She didn't forget the conversation either, I learned, when my husband came in from work saying, "Wow! What were you and Suzy talking about? She just rushed out yelling, 'You gotta come in quick! Mommy's going to grow me a baby and she needs your help to do it!' "

My way wasn't necessarily a good way to handle it—it just happened that way—and I remember getting a bit flustered trying to decide whether or not to include the "how." What would you have done? Would you have included intercourse? What would you have said had she asked for more detail? I got flustered mainly because I had assumed that her first question would be "How are babies born?" That it would come when we were rocking in the chair, and that I would tell her a charming little story. It never occurred to me that it would be on the run and that I wouldn't have time to pick and choose what I would say. At least I had thought about a general explanation, so even if I goofed, I wasn't too far from what I had planned.

Some books stop anticipating after they get through the "babies" part. Or for such issues as menstruation, they give long complicated answers, and forget to anticipate with readers what questions may have made such answers necessary. Once again, the assumption seems to be that parents will be able to sit down for a formal lesson in which they have carefully written down all the answers. I have noticed that when adult students in human sexuality classes write term papers on sex education, they are apt to copy answers from the textbook, with no attempt to rephrase them into conversational English. Under such circumstances they would have to memorize the words to repeat them and that would sound something less than human.

Here are some other questions and comments that various children of all ages have asked or given. It might help you to think about how you would answer them. Do try it out by talking out loud to yourself. Your comments have a way of sounding great when you are thinking them; it's only in voicing them that you realize where you may need to check your knowledge or attitudes. It will show you quickly that even the simplest question might be answered in several ways depending upon your basic attitudes.

"What's this? (tampon or sanitary napkin) What's it used for? Can I play with it? How do you use it? Can I watch you?"

These questions stymie a lot of people, especially when a child is too young for the whole story. Answering simply and directly is the best way. "It's a sanitary napkin." That usually satisfies a younger child, giving you time to think before he or she gets around to the next part, "What's it used for?" That too has an easy answer: "Menstruation." This answer may give you some breathing time. "Can I play with it?" has an obvious answer. What if the child asks, "Why not?" "Because it's private" will usually suffice. If you have a "why-er" on your hands, you'd better struggle with as many possible questions and answers as you can ahead of time. Obviously, you are making a trap for yourself that may be hard to get out of. You can avoid it by never allowing a first question if you are exceedingly clever, but anticipation can avoid a lot of getting out of traps. "Why is it private?" Because it is put on or inside the vagina which is a private part of our bodies." That also is an answer to "How is it used?" The next trap is apt to be "What's menstruation?" If the child is really young, you might say, "It's something that happens to all women once a month after they get to be around twelve or thirteen."

Usually young children will not push you that far. If the child is getting on towards ten years of age, you might want to use that as an opportunity for sitting down and giving him or her the whole story. No, it's not too young. Many girls start menstruating by ten, and can be frightened if they don't know what's happening to them. They think they've been hurt or are bleeding to death, and for some reason—I suspect masturbation—are afraid to tell anyone. You'd be amazed to know how many teenagers, even today who have just that experience. Also remember that boys as well as girls need the information.

Tip: You can fall into an unnecessary trap if you immediately assume a child needs the whole story. If you get too technical, you can get caught in some verbal Fallopian tubes and end having to say, "You're too young to understand." It should be apparent by now that the whole conversation will be much easier if you have already talked about intercourse and have used the words "uterus" and "vagina."

Tip: Sometimes in discussing babies or menstruation, I prefer the word "womb" to "uterus," partly because it's shorter, and partly because if you connect the word to a similar word, "room," it helps a little child to understand just what kind of a special place this is. Anything you can do to help a child visualize what he cannot actually see is useful.

Other questions children have asked:

Let's go on to some more questions children ask that have given parents trouble. Each one has been asked by youngsters of varying ages. I will indicate any time that I think the age at which one child asked might surprise you.

"Does having babies hurt?"

"What's intercourse? Does it hurt? How do you do it? Why do you do it?"

"What's making love?"

"What's petting?"

"What's a virgin?" (8 year old girl)

"What's rape?" (5 year old)

"What's 69?"

"Why is it that sometimes my penis is soft and little, and sometimes it's hard and rubbery?" (10 year old)

"How would you feel if I got pregnant?" (12 year old)

"Why shouldn't I talk to strangers? What would they do to me?"

"Why isn't it nice to show Johnny my vagina?"

"What's this?" (condom, diaphragm, birth control pills, etc.)

"I think Johnny's in love with me—he kissed me. What'll I do? I'm too young to get married. . .I didn't know what to do, so I kissed him back. Was that all right?" (11 year old girl)

"I heard a dirty joke today. Want to hear it?" (12 year old boy to mother).

"If you use birth control, is that killing a baby?"

"What's a blow job?" (11 year old)

"What's *Deep Throat* about? Why can't I see 'R-' and 'X-' rated movies?"

"What's sex?"

"Would it be okay if I wanted to have intercourse with a girl and I wanted to live with her, but I didn't want to get married? What would you say? Wouldn't it be better to try it out that way so that if one of us got tired of the other, we could leave?" (12 year old boy)

"Did you ever have sex before you were married?"

"How old were you the first time you had sex? Did you ever have sex with someone besides Mom (or Dad)?" (13 year old)

"What's masturbation?"

"Will boys like me if I don't have big breasts?"

"What will happen to me if my husband's penis is too big for me?"

"What's a prostitute?" (8 year old)

"Will I be able to have intercourse if my penis is small? Will a woman be disappointed?" (This one came from a 22-year old man about to be married.)

Here are some comments, mainly by teenagers, given to parents or counsellors:

"I wish I were a boy. Boys can ask girls for dates, girls have to sit and wait. And boys don't have periods. Boys don't have any worries."

"I want babies. But if it takes intercourse, I don't want to get married. Guess I'll have to adopt." (13 year old girl)

"I want to know more about venereal disease and birth control. But I'm afraid to ask my parents. And I'd be embarrassed to ask a doctor." (16 year old)

"I've had intercourse and I liked it. But I feel guilty because my parents don't know. Sometimes I think they know, but they won't admit it to themselves." (14 year old girl)

"I have sex with my fiance. I don't feel guilty about it, but I don't really like it. Neither does my married friend. What's wrong with us?" (19 year old girl)

"Parents don't realize the pressure there is to screw. Almost everyone in my classes has done it. I want to and I don't. And I don't want to be square, but I don't want to get a bad reputation either. I get so confused!" (14 year old girl)

"I don't really want to make out with girls sometimes, but you have to or the guys say you're queer. And the girls sometimes seem to expect it. How do you know what they want?" (16 year old boy)

"I won't ever have sex until I'm married. I think it's wrong. But boys seem to think it's a challenge to get me to do it. How can you say 'no' without making them mad or hurting their feelings?" (18 year old)

You can see with what a variety of questions and problems they need help. Some are easy to answer, some very difficult. Later on I'll give examples of conversations arising from some of these and other questions, and some sample explanations that can be used for terms like *vagina* and *menstruation*.* Remember, however, that your own explanations may be better than the ones I quote.

Adults often say to me, "Well, at least sex education is easy until adolescence because little children don't ask any profound questions." One such person in an adult class was dumbfounded when four of his friends reported similar questions by their seven year old children: "I thought you said our bodies were private. So why are there naked people in that magazine? And why do you look at them? And you said sex wasn't funny. So why do you laugh at the cartoons?" There wasn't a person in the class who could find a really adequate answer. Thus, while trying in vain to find a simple answer for the child's questions, the class members found themselves struggling with some important questions of their own.

Other people's children:

We have been talking about children for whom you have responsibility—mainly your own, but perhaps not. At least you probably don't plan to give sex education to anyone but your own child if you are a parent, your students if you are a teacher, or to those whom you are "helping," if you are a professional "helper." But you will be giving it—even to people you don't know. If you laugh at or walk out at a particular scene in a movie, you will be giving some information to the person sitting next to you. You will give even more unplanned information to people whom you know.

Here are some examples:

Many a young parent in a neighborhood with other young parents has grabbed a quick shower while the kids are out to play, and has stepped out of that shower to find a pair of beady eyes belonging to someone else's child gazing up at her or him.

Parents often take their children's friend along to a movie.

---

*See Appendix A.

If that movie has unexpected sexual content, those children will also be seeing or hearing it.

Children's friends are often in the house when your child is there, listening to conversations you have with adults or comments that you make to your own child.

Sometimes neighbors' children, nieces or nephews or others will ask you questions, either because you're there at the moment or because they're afraid to ask their own parents.

Children staying in your home will get the same education your own are getting. If they're of dating age, you may even have responsibility for their behavior.

The way in which you handle such situations will still depend upon your attitudes. They will be easier to handle if you have anticipated such problems.

Although one must use discretion in how one deals with other people's children, I try not to act too differently than I would with my own. If a question comes up, I try to answer it. If someone catches me disrobed, I grab for a towel, but I don't get in a tizzy; after all, he's the invader, not me. If I want to talk to my own child, I don't stop unless I think it will embarrass my child. I also use the same rules that I use in teaching: I refer the questioner back to his own parents for final authority, or for more elaborate discussion. If I think the situation warrants it, I call the child's parents, tell them what happened, and if necessary, ask their guidance on what to do in the future.

Adults:

Just because your child has reached adulthood and has had sexual experience, don't assume that questions or problems are over. Thinking of sex education only in terms of children is limiting. Many adults are badly in need of more accurate information. You will be providing information in either a planned or unplanned way to many adults, whether they are your children, your friends, relatives, or your parents.

You will provide attitudes in discussions and conversations. Sometimes you will have to deal with adult problem situations. Anticipating and exploring your own attitudes will be helpful here, as it was with your own small children. For example, how would you feel if your parents were to remarry? How do you feel about aged people acting like honeymooners? About older single people having sexual relationships?

Here are just a few questions or comments by adults:

"I feel guilty about masturbating. But what can I do? I still have needs even if I'm a widow. But I'm over 65. Who'd look at me?"

"I couldn't get an erection last night. Is my sex life over? Am I impotent?"

"I don't get an orgasm. Am I frigid?"

"How can my husband love me after a breast removal?"

"We're having lots of problems with sex. But we're embarrassed to ask the doctor. Pregnant people shouldn't be so concerned with sex."

"My children know more about sex than I do. But I'd feel silly talking to them. After all, I'm the parent."

"I'd like to talk to my folks. But I'm twenty-one. They'd think I was stupid."

Whether a person is one or ninety-one, questions and problems can arise and the need for adequate sex education remains.

Interjecting Humor:

Whether a situation involves adults or children, it helps to keep a sense of humor. First, some situations are really funny. Second, even though it's hard to explain humor to a child, you can teach through example. And third, sometimes you need your humor to see you through.

A father I know reported that once when he was standing naked in his bedroom, his small daughter and her friend burst into the room. They went over to him and stared, long and hard. Finally the daughter announced, "Joan's father has something like that on him, too. But her father's is much bigger than yours!"

A grandfather I know told a similar one: His granddaughter caught him, took a good look and then yelled into the next room, "Hey, Daddy! Grampa's got a penis too. But his is all broken!"

Remember children have a sense of humor, too. One talk show emcee tells about giving a long treatise on intercourse to his son. When he had finished, the son said, "Dad, I have just one question. "When you're 'doing it,' how do you keep from laughing?" I hope the answer was, "Sometimes we don't." Once after I had given a talk to retarded children about "How We Develop Into Adults," one youngster asked, "Well, how do people grow, anyhow?" Startled, I asked what he meant; his eyes held the proverbial twinkle as he said, "Well, I just thought maybe they went out in the back yard and watered themselves."

We talk about sex education with our own children, other people's children and adults. Sometimes we may find ourselves in a position where we are giving it to all three groups.

When my daughter was five, some friends and I took her along to a drive-in movie. Some unexpected things happened. First, the movie had a scene involving a teenage unmarried mother. Second, Suzy had not been bored and ready to go to sleep as I had expected, but watched intently throughout the film. Third, she understood more of the plot than I had expected her to.

On the way home she asked why everyone had been so mad at the girl. When told, she asked why having a baby was so bad, since I'd told her having babies was nice. It became obvious that I was getting into a difficult situation, but I anwered her questions one by one, and steeled myself for each new one. "Why shouldn't she have a baby so young?" "What was so bad? What had she done that was so wrong?"

I was acutely aware that my friends and their eight year old were listening. I did not know their views on sex, but I did know they were very religious. Moreover, I had two conflicting values. I wanted my children to know that intercourse was very important and not to be indulged in until people were responsible, and concerned for each other. I did not want her to feel that unmarried parents were inherently immoral. I had planned to talk about things like that with teenagers, not five year olds who had not yet asked about intercourse. I had certainly never planned to air my views in front of others or to give such attitudes to others' children.

I also felt I had to be consistent all the way through, and I should not wait until later to answer. So I cleared my throat, told her that in order to have babies, a man puts his penis inside a woman's vagina. Most people feel intercourse is very important and that they should wait until they are married. When she pressed me for an answer as to whether I thought it was wrong I said, "No, not exactly, but the girl had made a big mistake which had made her very unhappy, because she was too young and had not thought about it enough." I remember mentally clearing my throat a lot. Finally, we agreed that it was a bit hard to understand and we'd talk more about it in the future.

In retrospect, this conversation doesn't sound so difficult. What made it so at the time was the presence of others and the depth of the questions my daughter was asking, with decisions that needed to be made in a split second. It would have been much more difficult had I not at least thought about my values earlier. Of course my answer would have been profoundly different and easier had I believed that premarital sex was unequivocally wrong. The adults later confided to me that they had been highly relieved to hear my answer, partly because it had helped them decide what they would say to their daughter, and partly because they had been worrying about how I might react to knowing that they themselves had married during pregnancy.

With or without other people present, this conversation brings up one more point. One of the biggest difficulties was that Suzy had never gotten around to asking more about intercourse and I had been brought up on "Never answer until a child asks." This meant not only was I asking her to grapple with adult moral issues, but I also had to give her the basic, preliminary facts. The problem might have been eliminated had I realized that if a child has not asked those preliminary questions by the time he or she is four or five, and many don't, parents can make life easier by starting the ball rolling themselves. Many parents complain that no matter how willing they are, the child never asks them questions; they wonder if they have done something wrong. There is no point in worrying about it. The main thing to remember is that the more the child can talk with you, the more helpful you can be. There are many things you can do to get that conversation rolling and to keep it going. Those things are part of a general concept that I find crucial in giving sex education: the "Opening Doors Policy" in which you open and reopen doors.

CHAPTER FOUR

THE "OPENING DOORS POLICY"

The most useful sex education also involves a continual open-ing door policy. Whenever I use that term to adults, they brighten up and say, "Now you're making sense. I know what that means, but it's so obvious, why bother saying it? It means we tell the kids they should always feel free to ask questions, and then we will really try to answer them." That's part of it, but there is much more to an open door policy than that. Three non-sexual examples in everyday life come to mind.

Have you ever had a doctor say to you, "Now do you have any questions?" Sounded good, didn't it? But by the time you framed your question in your mind and opened your mouth to ask it, often as not the doctor already had one foot out the door. Either you decided he really didn't want you to ask, or that your question was so trivial you hated to detain him. He may have opened the door for you with his words, but he closed it with his actions.

Have you ever started a new job and had the boss say, "Now come in whenever you have a problem. My door is always open." Did you often take him up on that? Probably not after the first week, because you weren't sure what constituted a problem worth bothering a busy man, and you didn't want to look as if you couldn't cope. That boss opened the door an inch. But what was needed to make it a true open door policy was either for him to arrange a periodic conference that would "legalize" bringing up small problems casually, or for him to stop you in the hall occasionally and say, "Come in after lunch and let's talk about how things are going."

In social relationships how often have people said to you, "We must get together. Drop by any time, the coffee pot's always on." Do you act on that offer? Not unless you're sure that they really mean it. You won't be sure unless they call to make a definite date, call to chat, or drop in on you. Any one of those three things would be door openers necessary for a good, open door policy. Also, if someone extended an invitation to you for coffee, even if you did not like coffee, you would accept the invitation in order to open the door wider. Or if you could not make it, you would ask for a rain check, ask for another time, or make your own invitation in order to keep that door open.

The same thing is true in sex education. You can open a door once by saying, "Do you have any questions? If you ever do, feel free to ask." Chances are that a child won't be able to think of a question at the moment, will be too embarrassed to ask, or will not be sure you really mean it. So he or she will shut the door, and sometimes it won't get opened again unless you do the opening. A child may open a door an inch, but it will be up to you to open it wider and keep it open. Unlike a social situation when invitations refused two or three times may be permanent door closers that you may decide to accept, in sex education you will not want to accept a door closer as final.

A true open door policy means that you actively open the doors, keep on opening them; and when the child opens the doors, you open them even wider. Door openers are useful not only because of any discussion or factual information given at the moment, but because they provide information about attitudes and pave the way for future questions.

How do you go about opening doors?

There are countless ways to open doors, some simple and some more complicated. For instance, door openers can be as simple as allowing your child to see you undressed once in awhile. This experience gives information without saying a word, allows a child enough knowledge to know what questions are worth asking, and shows your attitude toward your body.

When I was a child, my mother never let me see her undress. When she wanted to do so and I was around, she went through a remarkable set of gyrations, pulling her blue nightgown over her and undressing under it. I used to stare in fascination, wondering what all those bumps and protrusions were, straining to catch a glimpse of what was under that nightgown, and convinced that if she went to all that trouble to keep me from seeing, it must indeed be worth seeing. Alas—she was too good for me; I never saw a thing. Although she thought she was open with me by telling me about menstruation and where babies come from, she never thought to mention pubic hair. The result? It never occurred to me that women grew hair. The first time I took a fleeting peek at a woman in a public bathhouse, I was horrified. It looked to me in that moment (and of course my mother had taught me without words, that it wasn't nice to really look) that the woman was covered with hair. I suppose I thought she was turning into a werewolf, and how could I ask my mother about it later? I didn't think of it as "sexual," but I had obviously been looking at forbidden sights.

My mother never meant to give me those ideas, she just did. Later, when I found a few strands of hair on myself, although I had forgotten all about the woman, I was frightened. What was happening to me? Was it something bad? Luckily, I spent the night with a girl friend soon after. She was not so reticent about "looking," and proudly showed me her few strands. When I looked down and saw that those hairs had a name that meant "growing up," I was mightily relieved. My mother's unwillingness to open such a door did not scar me for life. But had she opened it, I could have been saved a bit of panic and come to her more easily with questions when I had them. This example has an added moral: You need not be too concerned if your children explore their bodies with other children, as they will. It won't hurt them and it may as it did in my case, help them. You will not remember to tell them everything any more than my mother did. Exploration can fill in the gaps.

Door openers are the exact opposite of the rule "Never answer until a child asks," a rule started in the thirties and forties because "liberal" parents thought they had to give long lectures to their children, and sometimes jumped the gun. Out of that situation came a story about the child who asked where he came from, got a half hour treatise on the birds and the bees, and then said disgustedly, "Yeah, but Johnny comes from Ohio. I wanna know where I come from." From that kind of story came the rule which is to a certain extent common sense. Let's change the wording of the rule to *"Make sure you know what your child is asking before you answer it, and don't feel you have to get in all the information at once."*

In addition, long lectures can be a way of avoiding the subject. Not only do they bore a child, but also by fancy terminology and long paragraphs you can suggest to a child that you are afraid to talk about sex, and that sex is something of which to be afraid.

My mother goofed in that area, too. Poor Mom! She tried so hard. Her explanations were so long and intellectual that I tuned out in two minutes. The only thing I ever understood out of an hour's discussion about menstruation was that some day I would find blood in my underwear and I shouldn't worry about it. That was good enough for me. My older sister though, hadn't fared so well. She hadn't understood a word, and when she began to menstruate, she was as frightened as if she'd never been told anything. I did, however get two bits of unplanned sex education. I learned that my mother found it uncomfortable to talk about sex; and hence, it must be an uncomfortable subject. Because I loved my mother and did not want to embarrass her any more than I wanted to feel embarrassed myself, I directed any questions to my sister from then on.

The last two examples were extremes of "no information" and "too much information." With door openers there are many "middle of the road" ways to deal with sex information. When my daughter was two or three, she came into the room when my husband and I were undressed, and eye level with my husband's penis, she stared and stared. I started to say something, but since I tend to be one of the "gun-jumpers," my husband reminded me that she would ask when ready. The next day it happened again. The third day my husband began to get rather uncomfortable. I finally said to myself, "That's silly. If she were staring at his finger, we would say, 'You want to know what that is? It's a finger.' " Out loud I said, "You want to know what that is? It's a penis."

My daughter said matter of factly, "Oh." She repeated the word to herself once, left the room and went to play with her dolls. The next day there was no coming into the room, and no staring.

That was a door opener. Now I could have gone on; I might have added, "all men have one." But I didn't need to, and a long explanation when she was obviously satisfied would have been pointless. That door opener took two minutes, answered a question, gave her a bit of vocabulary, and let her know that it's all right to be curious.

Door openers, then, don't have to wait until children reach the "right" age, or ask. To wait for that is like saying we'll wait to teach them to speak until they're already talking, or we won't talk to them until they've learned how. Of course that's silly. We start talking to babies long before they know how to talk— that's how they learn.

If we want to teach children about God, we don't wait until they've entered theological seminary—we don't even wait until they know what God is. We stand with them and watch a rainbow, and say, "What a beautiful rainbow God made." Or we have them fold their hands at bedtime and say a prayer. They don't have the vaguest idea what it's all about, but eventually they think about it and ask, "What's God?" When someone mentions the word in school then, they don't fall over with silliness and fright as children often do in school when someone mentions "sex." Yet somehow when it comes to sex, we assume that without the vocabulary and familiarity with words, and with attitudes developed through what is *not* said, they will suddenly wake up and be able to carry on a relaxed, warm, comfortable discussion about very complicated material. That doesn't make much sense, does it?

Tip:

If you carry on that homework assignment about discussing values with your husband or wife while your children are around, even if they don't enter into the conversation, you will have opened a door both with your words and your attitudes. If nothing else, they will learn that sex is a discussable item in your house not because you told them it was, but because you are showing them.

Some more sample door openers:

Perhaps your little boy is just learning how to talk, or is

even younger. Notice that as you bathe him, you are apt to say "Now let's clean your hands," "Now let's clean your face," etc. Or you will teach him his body parts: "Here are your eyes," "this is your nose," "show me your hands." Many people teach children every part of their body except the genitals, or if they mention such areas, they do it in a "special" context, in a "special" way. If you just include the word penis, or vagina, with no more and no less emphasis than any other part, both the words and the body parts take on less emotional charge and become just what they were meant to be, part of a general body of knowledge requiring no special lecture. It can save you a lot of time and embarrassment, making life much easier when you want to talk about more complicated subjects that require knowledge of those basic terms.

You teach your children, through story books, about many things that are unfamiliar to them. They learn about dogs, lions or fire trucks even before they can speak, just by seeing pictures in a book or hearing a story you make up. They probably do not understand most of what you're saying, and enjoy the warmth of reading with you, hearing your voice, seeing bright pictures. Bit by bit they recognize the words, and learn about many complicated things without a big fuss.

For some reason, books about sex are usually left out. They are made a special deal, and when the children finally get the story it is with a lot of new words all at once, and hence mysterious and hard to comprehend. If you slip in a story book about babies, or even if you make one up, they do not need to understand it at first—eventually it will become a favorite story like other stories.

It isn't hard to make one up for a three year old; let me make one up right now:

"Once upon a time there was a little egg no bigger than a dot. It lived inside a mother, right about here. It was snug and cozy and warm. One day it began to grow. Every day it got a little bigger and a little bigger, and parts of it began to grow lumpy. All of a sudden, pop!—one of those lumps looked like a head. And then another lump looked like a leg, and then came another leg, and then some arms. And then it grew some eyes and ears, and a nose and mouth, and hair. And all the time it was growing bigger and bigger. Pretty soon it began to get cramped. "My," it said to itself "this house is too small. I want to get out and have room to play." So it wriggled and pushed until it found an opening between the mother's legs, and worked and worked, and suddenly, POP, there it was out in the open. And it had brown hair and brown eyes, and it looked so cute, its mother hugged and hugged it. Do you know what it looked like? It looked like you. You know why? That's right, because it was you. It was a baby, and the mother was me, and Daddy and I named you_____, and we were so proud!"

That wasn't too hard, was it? You might start with "Do you know what you were like a long time ago? You were no bigger than a dot." It might even be an offshoot of the many times you say to a child, "My, how big you are." You might grab a crayon and draw as you talk. Your children might not understand half of it. But the fun of learning about themselves, especially if there's a surprise ending, will probably excite them no end. You stand a good chance of it being their favorite story, and with each telling you can add a fact painlessly. What if the children aren't interested? Who cares? You have opened the door, you can always reopen it whenever you wish, and they will walk through it when they want to.

Some quickie door openers:

Suppose your teenagers say, "Wow! There's a girl in school who's going to have a baby!" You can ask how they know or what they think about it, or what the kids are saying about it. They have opened the door a crack—by encouraging them to talk more about it, you are opening it wider.

Supposing you are washing dishes and just happen to think about how big your son or daughter is getting, and that soon you will need to talk about nocturnal emissions, menstruation, or dating. You can just say, "You know, I was just thinking about some of the changes that are going to start taking place in your body pretty soon—maybe we should talk about them before they happen, so you'll know what to expect." He or she may want to take you up on that right away and then again, maybe not. But you have opened the door. Suppose you're explaining something to an older son and your younger one is around. Do you send the younger one away? Not if you're a "door opener." The younger one may chime in, sit and listen, or just daydream while you're talking. But he will learn—either specific information or an attitude. If you say, "Perhaps you have questions too, or will in the future," you will keep the door open for him.

You can leave tampons or a package of condoms around. You can say, "Whoops, excuse me, I think I just started my period," instead of rushing off quietly to take care of things. If you are a husband, you can ask your wife if her period has started yet.   Or you can let your youngster buy your supplies occasionally. That way, the words are familiar and the subject is more comfortable whenever he or she wishes to ask about it, or you wish to discuss it. Also, even though you may be unable to prevent the acute embarrassment that many teenagers feel when making their first purchase for themselves, you will have gone a long way in easing that feeling.

Some things to remember about door openers:

They can start when the child is an infant and go on forever.

They can be both verbal and non-verbal.

They can range from one-worders to full blown discussions.

They can be non-reactions. For example: not reacting when a child yells "fuck" to get a rise out of you, or not rushing to cover yourself when a child pops in on you.

They can allow you to let some things happen which you might have tried to prevent. For example: leaving some magazines or books about sex around instead of hiding them, leaving contraceptive devices around once in a while instead of putting them away, using a four-letter word occasionally instead of carefully avoiding it.

They can answer two or three questions at once, giving information about "unasked" questions as well as "asked" ones.

When a boy asked why his penis got hard or rubbery, his parents answered this way: "First of all it's a natural part of growing up that will happen more and more as you get older." That was because they thought an unasked question was "Am I normal?   Is anything wrong?"   Then they added, "Sometimes it happens when boys have to go to the bathroom, and sometimes it occurs when boys masturbate: that means when they feel their penis. As you get older it will also happen when you're thinking about girls, or at night when you're dreaming about girls. It happens to all boys and men." That answer took care of two topics, erection and masturbation. It paved the way for talking about nocturnal emissions, and also, because both parents participated, it let him know that both were willing to discuss things.

Notice that they used the word "when" instead of "if" when talking about masturbation. That was because they thought he might be worried that masturbation was harmful or wrong; but they didn't want to put him on the spot. They assumed that like most children he was doing it; they let him know their attitude, and gave him information without any big discussion. His nod when they mentioned masturbation let them know that they were on the right track, without his having to "admit" anything. This whole discussion took place in about two minutes while getting dressed for work and school. By telling him that he might have more questions about it that they'd be glad to answer when they were not so rushed, they kept the door open for the future.

Two added thoughts about door openers:

Just because you have opened a door once, don't think that you'll never need to open it again.

Children, as well as adults, have a way of forgetting; the more complicated the material, the more apt they are to forget part of it. One door opener that can be useful is to tell children every so often that if they forget, they can ask again. Forgetting has its compensations. It gives you second chances if you've goofed and second chances work two ways: If you've forgotten something, you needn't hesitate to bring it up again, either. All you need to do is say, "By the way, when we were talking the other day, I forgot to mention...."

If you get caught at a bad time, and there's only time to make a brief comment and say, "I'll talk to you about it later," that's okay. But remember to do so!

Children often forget the "facts" they have been told, and parents often forget their "promises." It's the parents' responsibility to remember the "promise" and keep the door open. Don't expect the children to remind you just because you told them to. They probably won't. They'll be apt to assume that was just a "door closer."

Door closers:

We've talked a lot about door openers; what about door closers? Here are a few:

"You are too young to understand."

This is probably the most famous and most often used door

closer. It seems to close doors more effectively than any other.
I would try never to say it. If there are times when the topic
really seems too difficult for the child to understand, what do you
do then? Stop and think for a moment. Any child who asks a
question is old enough for an answer. Is the problem because the
child is too young? Or, is it because you have not determined
how to answer it without confusing or frightening the child?
So, why not simply say, "That's a good question. I'm not sure I
know the answer to it—let me think about it a bit and then we'll
talk more about it." Or another way of handling it might be to
try to answer it until you see that the child is getting confused,
and then you can say, "It's hard to understand, isn't it. Don't
worry, we'll talk more about it from time to time. The older you
get the easier it will be to understand." See how easily you can
change a door closer to a door opener?

Some more door closers:

*Telling a child, "Go ask your father or mother," or saying,
"Don't bother me now, I'm busy."*

*Demanding an accounting of the child's behavior the minute
he or she asks about some sexual behavior.*

You may need to eventually open the door to the possibility
that your child may be trying to tell you something. But jumping
to that conclusion closes the door—not only does it close the door,
it may slam it shut. How can a child discuss ideas if he or she feels
that it will lead to an immediate accusation of wrongdoing?

*Making a "yuk" sound or face or making a strong statement
about a controversial subject before the child has had a chance to
voice his or her opinions.*

Having sworn never to talk to my mother again about sex, I
tried once more. We were discussing a girl friend of mine, whom
she considered the epitome of sweetness, purity, beauty and intel-
lect. I, being a bit jealous, mentioned the one thing that I sensed
would not please Mother, while trying a tentative door opener on
a subject with which I myself was struggling. I told her my friend
was known to be a heavy "petter." Mother made a horrible face,
shuddered, and said in a shocked tone, "I can't believe it! How
could anyone let a man paw her like an animal? Ugh!"

I got what I had been looking for. Mother never again compared me to that girl, and I got my feedback about petting. That
was the last time sex was mentioned between us until the day I

married, when Mother worriedly noted our lack of communication and wondered if I had any questions. She was considerably relieved that I felt I knew everything, and I was considerably relieved that she never thought of asking "how come."

Clinchers.

There are times, however, when a response that cuts off discussion can be useful. I call such responses "clinchers"—they confirm (clinch) an attitude you have already given, rather like adding an exclamation point to the end of a sentence. Hence even though they may limit further discussion, they are not door closers in the negative sense that we have just mentioned. For example, if you have already talked about a controversial subject in various ways, you're quite sure that the child understands and is not trying to open a door, but is merely testing out whether you meant what you said earlier, an impulsive reaction might be the best thing you could give.

My children and I have talked about premarital sex and pregnancy at various times, in relation to their announcement that a girl in school was pregnant. At first I avoided strong statements until their opinions were out in the open. This led to a discussion with my daughter of, "How would you feel if I..." As the schoolmate progressed in the pregnancy, conversation about it occurred casually. One day, however, my daughter said to me, "I think I know how you'll answer this, but our teacher told us to ask our parents. How do you feel about my being in a school where there's a pregnant girl? Would you want her removed?"

I didn't stop to analyze—I exploded with anger at a school which would even consider such a possibility. Then I remembered my own rule, and suggested that she might have a different opinion. She said, "Oh, Mother," in the scornful voice that only the parent of a teenager will recognize, paused a moment, and then said, smiling, "That's what I told her you'd say."

My impulsive answer here "clinched" earlier discussions, confirming my attitude that while premarital sex for young girls may not be wise, it does not render the girl inherently evil. However, it also became a door opener for a wider range of topics. My daughter went on to ask, "Is it okay if I act 'normal' toward her?" I said, "Of course! How else?" "Would you mind if I was friends with her?" When it came to "friends," we began to discuss how I felt about any friends she might choose—worries I had as a parent, and faith I had in her as a daughter.

This brings up the point that not only are there many ways of reacting to one situation, the same statement may be a door opener in one situation and a door closer in another. Your decision on how to react will depend on what you think is going on. Sometimes you might even need to ask. If your son has asked the same question over and over, for instance, you might mention that fact and ask if there's something else that's bothering him.

Some homework:

Try to think of some times in your own life when you used or might have used some door openers on a particular subject. Think about some possibilities for the future. Remember, there is only one limit to the number and kinds of door openers you can use, and that is the limit of your imagination.

Serendipity:

Somehow people seem to limit themselves to opportunities that they themselves have created or that are directly and obviously part of sex education. So I like to extend door opening to a concept called "serendipity," which allows you to make the most of opportunities created by accidental events or situations that at first glance would not seem part of your planned sex education program.

First, let's talk about serendipity. Despite variations in the use and meaning given to it, it is used in science when referring to a useful scientific discovery made as the result of some accident. This is not the same as an accidental discovery; scientific discoveries do not lie around in pure form waiting to be noticed, and not all accidental discoveries are serendipitous.

To fit the requirements of serendipity, the discoverer must have a basic interest in a particular subject, and enough knowledge about it to recognize the hidden potential of an "accident." Putting together knowledge and interest, he or she develops an automatic eye for seeing unusual possibilities that are often missed. Louis Pasteur perhaps put it best in a famous saying, ". . .chance favors the prepared mind." Only when the discoverer really *does* something to turn that accident into something more useful, can it finally be called serendipity.*

*The history of this term is in itself a good illustration of its meaning. Derived from an old legend, it was coined by Walpole in the 1700's, picked up by the physical, industrial, and social sciences in the 1950's, and has since even been used to name a popular singing group. Thus it has continually been discovered in one form, recognized

There are two common examples used to explain the difference between "accident" and "serendipity."

Remember that old tale about the caveman who dropped his raw meat into the fire accidentially and then ate it? Finding that it tasted good, he started the tradition of cooking meat. That was not serendipity; he did not change his discovery in any way through any interest or knowledge, but merely repeated an accident that had paid off.

When Madame Curie was doing research on radioactivity in uranium, she discovered a new substance that was even more highly radioactive than uranium itself. She named this substance radium, and recognizing its potential, she turned her attention to it and learned how to make it useful in treating disease. This was called serendipity, because she had both interest and knowledge in the subject matter, recognized the potential of her "accident," and turned it into something more useful.

Similarly, I have often walked along Hawaii's beaches idly picking up shells. Occasionally I'd notice a round one with a puka (hole) in the middle of it, say "how interesting," and then throw it away. But mothers with an eye out for ways of keeping their children amused had their children string such shells into a necklace. Eventually someone with an eye for business opportunities sold some necklaces to tourists, starting a puka shell necklace fad that swept the country, earning himself and many others a great deal of money.

What does all this have to do with sex education? If you start off with a basic interest or plan in sex education plus a bit of knowledge, you will have a "prepared mind," ready to turn all sorts of accidental events into door openers.

Examples:

Right now you are reading a book. It may be about sex education in general, but it is not specifically and directly part of the education you are planning to give your child. It is an "accident." But supposing you take a particular idea from it, and at supper tonight you say to your family,

"I'm reading an interesting book. One of the things it says is that sex education in schools should be taught with boys and

for its potential, and modified to make it useful in another way. I, too, have treated it as my "accident," and modified it for use in education.

girls in the same class. I'm not sure I agree. What do you think, Dad? How do you feel about that, Tommy?"

You have turned that accident into a door opener.

Supposing you go to a club meeting and hear a lecture on women's liberation. You certainly didn't think of it as sex education. But if you come home and say,

"I heard an interesting lecture about women today. One point the speaker made was that women will not be free sexually until they decide what is right and enjoyable for themselves as individuals, instead of trying to live up to others' expectations. She also said that men are no freer than women in that respect. What do you think about that?"

Even if your children are too young to have an opinion, just your discussion with your husband and your asking the question will have turned that lecture into a door opener.

Here is another one. You have probably seen pregnant women on the street dozens of times without giving them more than a passing glance. They remain "accidents." Suppose, however, that today you're walking with your four-year-old son who has never asked a question. You are not particularly disturbed about that, but you have a basic interest and plan in sex education, and at least some basic knowledge. Today when you see a pregnant woman crossing the street, inspiration suddenly hits you. You say to your child in a close, confidential whisper, "See that lady? I don't know her, but I know something special and nice that's going to happen to her soon. Would you like to know what it is?" Hopefully he will say, "Yes! Tell me quick!" There you are; you have turned that accident into a serendipitous bit of sex education.

What if he's not the least bit interested, and is more concerned about the fire engine in the next block? You can drop the subject entirely if it seems best, or you can just say casually, "She's going to have a baby; there's a good story about babies, remind me to tell you some day." Then you turn your attention to the fire engine in the next block.

Of course it might be just your luck to have him say scornfully, "She's pregnant. What's so special about that?" When you get over feeling deflated, you might recognize that at least you now know why he never asks questions of you—he is getting answers from someone else. It might be a good idea to know who that someone is, and what other things he is learning. You might say in a pleased voice, "I didn't know you knew that, that's pretty good! Who told you?" After you find out a little more, you might comment that even though you're glad he's asking questions and learning things, sometimes mothers of other children have different ideas than you do, or the children get mixed up. So you hope he'll remember to ask you, too.

The reason for sounding pleased is that if you make him feel guilty about talking with others, you won't prevent him from doing so, but you may prevent him from checking out answers with you. You may prefer that he talk with you in the first place, but you can honestly be glad that he has the spirit to seek information wherever he can, and that he is at least sharing that immediate knowledge with you now.

You have probably used pregnancy as a serendipitous accident without even thinking about it, if you have two children, or even one and a half. You don't have to limit yourself to your own pregnancy. You can ask a friend to let your child feel her stomach if you don't have a pregnant one of your own on hand. Then the three of you can start chatting about where babies come from.

Suppose there just happens to be a television special on sex, pregnancy, venereal disease, or something else interesting? Don't be afraid to watch it while the children are around, or even to suggest that they watch too. If it's too old for them, they'll be bored, or not pay too much attention. They may walk in or out, or play a game. But your attitude will teach them something, and that accidental bit of programming will become a door opener.

Sometimes there's not much difference between serendipity and door openers. If you're watching a movie or television program and there's an unexpected scene, that in itself is a door opener, because it may stimulate a question or give some information. If you initiate conversation or make a comment, you have already taken it a step farther and made it more useful. For instance, a common scene is one of people preparing hot water for childbirth, or seeing a woman in labor screaming. You might say to a child, "That makes having a baby sound kind of mysterious and scarey, doesn't it! I'm sure glad nowadays we make it a lot easier to have babies." Or you might just comment to no one in particular that you think the movie is exaggerating the amount of pain.

An important worry that many parents have about door openers and serendipity:

This worry has to do with "risk." With all these door openers and seizing opportunities, is there a real danger that you can expose children to too much before they are ready, and harm them instead of help them? Aren't you cramming needless information into them?

Yes, there is risk, but more for the parent than for the child. You risk the probability that you will get into traps, as I did in the drive-in movie. You will make errors, because you don't have control over what comes next, once you open a door, and you may get into a question or problem before you've figured out how to deal with it. I suspect that sensing this is what keeps some people from ever starting. You run such risks, however, whether you open doors or not; you actually have more control when you open the door than you do just waiting for some question to come popping out of the blue.

As to the risk for children—whether they will be exposed to material too early and be upset or harmed by it, again such risks occur whether you open doors or not. In fact, any upset you might unintentionally cause is apt to be far less dangerous than the kind of misinformation children receive while they are alone or with their peers. After all, you will be sensitive to and concerned about their reactions, and committed to helping them further. Other people may not be.

Most children, if they are not ready for sexual material, will merely be bored by it and will tune it out. They will pick up only what they are ready for and able to comprehend. All the more reason for you to reintroduce the subject at various times, to tell children that if it gets confusing, you will talk about it again when they are older and they'll be able to understand better.

Naturally, some common sense and discretion need to be used. If your children go with you to every movie with violent sex and see nothing about sex but violence, they'll think all sex is violent. Even in comedies, they may misinterpret because they don't understand the nuances that make sexual scenes funny. If you pick up every possibility for a door opener that you see, they will be so sick of sex that they will turn you off when you most want them to listen. If you deliver half-hour lectures every time they ask a simple question, you'll bore them to death, and they'll turn to anyone but you. You'll have turned door openers into door closers.

The thing to remember is that you're opening doors and inviting them through, not pushing them through whether they want to go or not. They will decide whether to make use of the opportunity; but whether they do or not, you will have been helpful to them merely by letting them know that the opportunity exists.

CHAPTER FIVE

"HELP! WHAT DO I DO NOW?"

AVOIDING OR GETTING OUT OF TRAPS

In order to be able to talk to people about sensitive problems, psychologists and social workers use some basic techniques of interviewing. They are really nothing more than extensions of common sense and basic human feelings; you have probably used them automatically almost every day. They include those rules that I questioned at the beginning of the book such as "be warm" and "be honest." Despite my dislike of the glib way in which they are constantly put forth, they are basic to any sex education and some thoughts about them, along with some tips and exercises in communication, will make it easier to avoid and recover from errors and traps.

If you sometimes get all choked up and cotton-mouthed after you've cleared your throat, STOP, RELAX, AND THINK! What are you trying to do? Answer every conceivable question perfectly like a computer? Of course not! All you really want to do is let children know that you understand some of the problems and worries they are having or will have; that you love them, and want to do anything you can to help ease their anxieties. If you can communicate that to them, you need not worry so much about what you say at the moment and they will not really expect much more from you. If you feel later you haven't handled a question or situation as well as you might have wished you will have made it possible to bring it up again.

The difficulties, of course, are that sometimes you really *won't* understand how they feel, sometimes they won't *think* you do unless you can find a way to show them, and sometimes you will require their additional help *in order* to really understand. The process of sharing thoughts and feelings is called communication, and is an important part of helping people deal with problems. It requires warmth, empathy (understanding) and honesty no matter what the problem or age of the person with whom you are dealing; this holds true for parents, teachers, counsellors, doctors, friends, spouses, or for any situation in which one person is trying to be helpful to another. Unfortunately, warmth, empathy and honesty are so interwoven in communication that it becomes difficult to separate them. But let's try.

Empathy starts with really listening to what someone is saying, trying to figure out what that person is feeling. It doesn't mean you have to agree with that person or feel the same way, it merely requires understanding how he or she does feel, and perhaps why. You can often understand the "why" by remembering times when you have felt similarly, even though the situation and feelings may have not been exactly the same.

Being warm means showing in some way, not necessarily verbally that you understand. If you really understand, you will avoid making mistakes in how you handle the situation.

Here's an example: A teenage boy mooning over unrequited love says to his mother, "I'm so in love with Barbara, I'll never get over it, not ever!" Does Mother, with the experience of age, say, "Oh, that's just Puppy Love. You'll get over it in no time." Not if she's got empathy, she doesn't. She thinks back to the time when she felt that way about someone and remembers what a strong feeling it was. Then she says something like, "I know. I went through that once too. You just can't think about anything else, and your stomach gets tied up in knots. Well at least that's the way it was with me. Is it the same with you? It's rough! I wish I could help more, but at least I know the way you feel." Perhaps she puts her arm around him. After he has gone through it a time or two, she may wish to comment that like other people who have felt that way, he will get over it eventually. Such reassurances will fall on empty ears, however, unless she has first proved that she really and truly understands that love is love, no matter how temporary it might be, and that he is suffering.

Of course there are times when a child will be completely baffling. You never felt the way he or she does. Do you bluff it through and say "I understand" anyhow? Here is where honesty comes in. Guesswork can get you into a terrible trap, and you mustn't promise more than you can deliver. All you can really promise is that if the child will try to share the problems with you, you will really try to understand. You will show real warmth and empathy at times by saying honestly, "Well, John, I'm not sure I understand completely, because I felt so differently when I was your age. But try to explain to me again. I want to help, and I remember how alone I felt and how exasperated I got when my father didn't understand what I was trying to tell him."

Right there you have used empathy, if only by recognizing the feelings he might be having at that very moment. You have proved your willingness to try harder. That's what he wants. Eventually, or perhaps right away, he'll try harder to help you.

Here is some homework to do:

Sit down and try to remember some of the worries and confusions that you had when you were your child's age. Remember especially the way you felt whenever an adult said, "Well, when I was your age. . . ." Which adult memories pleased you and which ones angered you? You'll probably find a number of little things you'd forgotten that will make your own child more understandable.

Some communication exercises and games you can play with your family, friends, or students:

Most communication problems start because people don't really listen to each other. Try *really* listening to someone expound for two minutes on something meaningful to him or her. Listen so hard that in two minutes you'll be able to repeat back word for word, tone for tone what has just been said. Do not try to understand what is in the speaker's head; do not think about how you will answer or what you will talk about when your turn comes; do not think about whether you agree or disagree, and do not try to anticipate the end of the story. Just listen and repeat. You'll be surprised at how hard it is to do. After you have repeated let your partner tell you how well you did, and where you missed. You might discover that you got the words right, but over or underemphasized them. Share with your partner any difficulties you had in keeping your mind from wandering. Then switch roles and let your partner do the listening.

The second exercise is similar to the first, but this time, look for what's in your partner's mind. Don't worry about the words so much; what's important is how your partner is feeling. Is he or she happy? Sad? Scared? Irritated? Furious? Why? What is written between the lines? If you get it fairly right, that's empathy.

These exercises are sometimes easier to do in groups of three, where one person can act as timer and observer, and share observations with the others.

For the next exercise, take turns expressing your feelings about a situation or person. The listener tries to remember a situation that was similar, and checks out whether or not the feelings were nearly the same. If not, the speaker explains again, and they keep going until the speaker is satisfied that the listener really understands.

If you can at least empathize with feelings, you won't feel so helpless when you don't know how to answer or help.

Honesty

Despite my beginning remarks, honesty is almost always the best policy. You may, however, need to redefine what you are being honest about. Here are some situations in which problems of honesty come into play. Suppose you get caught in a conversation with your son which embarrasses you no matter how much you try to hide it. The more you tell yourself to relax, the more uncomfortable you get and the more you stumble over your words. Do you go on stumbling your way through?

Be more comfortable about discomfort. You can get out of that trap easily with a bit of honesty, mixed perhaps with a bit of humor. Try stopping in the middle of a stumble, laughing at yourself, and being honest about your obvious discomfort. Then explain why. Perhaps it's because you can't figure out what words to use. Perhaps it's because you got caught with your knowledge down, or because your upbringing did not allow talking about sex. Let your son know that embarrassment is your hangup and not his, or that it comes from the situation itself, rather than from being embarrassed about sex itself, and that you'll stumble through if he'll just bear with you. You'll find that both of you become considerably less embarrassed quite soon.

You can even mimic yourself, dramatize difficulty with a particular word, practice saying it together— anything to get you both laughing and ease the tension. These techniques accomplish many goals. You let your son know that difficult situations can be worked out if people keep trying; you give *him* permission to be embarrassed and hence to feel less alone; you keep doors open and you become closer in the process of sharing feeling; you are a good model for parenthood because you are showing that parents can be honest and human.

Suppose you are ambivalent about a moral issue such as unwed pregnancy or premarital sex. If you give one viewpoint, you fear you'll scare your child out of ever coming to you with a problem. If you give the other, you're afraid he or she will consider it a license to be irresponsible. Do you close your eyes and pick? You can, adding an afterthought with the qualifying statements. Or you can just be honest. You can say, "I don't know what to tell you. If I sympathize with an unwed mother, I'm afraid you'll think I condone premarital sex. But if I say I do not approve of premarital sex, I worry that you'll be afraid to come to me for help if you ever need to. I want you to know how I feel about it, but I also want you to know that I would always try to understand any problem you might have, and I'd never want you to be afraid to come to me for help."

You can even answer "what if's" more easily in that way. For instance, "What if I got pregnant?" It's pointless to say you'd be all understanding if you know perfectly well you'd be very upset and angry. Chances are you don't know how you'd react. So why not say so? You'd probably try to get beyond anger and hurt to try to understand and help. So you can and should say that, too. Some parents and teachers are so afraid that they'll be classed old-fashioned or uptight that they won't give opinions about anything. This can leave young people confused, frightened and uncertain as to what you really want for them, and maybe even unsure that you really care for them.

I once answered a "what if" about pregnancy with values about "understanding." My daughter was highly relieved. "I'm so glad you wouldn't kick me out," she said, "like my friend's mother did." I mentally patted myself on the back. Then she added, "I'm so glad you wouldn't care." There was a moment of dumbfounded silence, and then I said, "Now wait a minute! I never said I wouldn't care!" Then we began to discuss more honestly the worry, the guilt, the anger that I would have. I believed what I first said, and I would never retract it. I don't really think I gave her a message like "I wouldn't care." But if that's all she heard, I obviously hadn't conveyed to her all I wanted to convey.

You should be honest about your own values; but you should also acknowledge the fact that others may disagree. There is nothing wrong with saying, "It may be old-fashioned, uptight, or even wrong. But that's how I feel." Hopefully, you won't always expect children to agree with you, even though you may at times need to insist that they obey you. Disagreement with them won't mean you lose respect for them. In the same way, children don't always need your agreement; they can respect you for what you are, if you can respect them for what they are.

Honesty does not mean you have to answer every question asked, or volunteer every bit of information that you have. If a question is an invasion of your privacy, or if you don't think an answer will be helpful, you can be honest about not wanting to answer as long as you explain why. Your honesty and your insistence upon your own rights is sex education in itself. You are the model for their behavior. You are a better model when you are honest about your feelings than when you are hedging or lying your way through an answer. Just remember your own feelings if your child at some point insists on his own right to privacy, and try not to assume that it's an insult to you or a symptom of wrongdoing.

Tips on how to talk about sensitive subjects:

Professionals, in order to obtain information they need, or to help people talk without giving them a third-degree, quickly learn the art of asking questions without asking questions. You have probably used their techniques often without realizing it. In order to understand what your child's real concern is, you will want him or her to tell you as much as possible with as little interrogation on your part as possible.

Avoid questions that can be answered "yes" or "no" or in one word. This is because "yes-no" questions imply a right or wrong answer, and people feel put on the spot. Unsure of what is the "right" answer, they will answer what they think you want to hear. *Example:* "Do you masturbate?" "Do you worry about sex?" "Do you hate your mother?" "Do you ever rob the cookie jar?" Also, even if you get an honest answer or a one word reply what good does it do you? You have to ask another question and another, and a third-degree ensues.

Try for an open-ended questions or comments. "I guess you're pretty mad at your mother. Maybe you could tell me about it." "I wonder if you're asking about masturbation; maybe we could talk about it. I imagine that you might have a lot of questions."

Even if there have to be some "yes- no's" along the way, it leaves people free to elaborate by themselves and you need fewer questions. Now try this one: "You know, most people think a lot about sex, and especially at your age, many people worry a lot about it. I imagine you might, too. And a lot of people are pretty embarrassed talking about it. But it's important to get straight answers. Maybe you could tell me about some of the things you or the kids you know worry about." That speech combines empathy by showing understanding of possible feelings like worry and embarrassment, with an open-ended question, using another idea, the *many people* concept.

Many people feel that they are the only ones who think or act a certain way. This makes them feel terribly alone— abnormal— and beyond anyone's understanding. Such worries are universal no matter what the age and apply to many situations other than sex. "Yes- no" questions then make them even more fearful and vulnerable. If you start out by letting them know that they are not alone in the particular thought or behavior which you want to discuss, and that it is not a question of trying to make them admit something, they will feel relieved no matter what their answer might be. They may then be able to talk more honestly and comfortably.

While this technique is designed to help put people more at ease in general discussions, it can be especially useful if you are ever worried that your children are in trouble and afraid to tell you. It helps you open the door without making accusations.

This does not mean jumping to conclusions, it just admits possibilities. You do not have to say *many people*; any opening which seems appropriate and comfortable to you and lets them know they are not alone will do. In the speech above, the child was given an "out" whereby he or she could talk about problems in the third person using as examples friends at school. Many people need such a device before they can be comfortable discussing such ideas about themselves.

When you use these concepts, you are doing more than freeing people to talk. You are giving useful information even if the conversation goes no farther.

If you make use of a general assumption about human behavior, you may find you can use *many people* concepts more automatically and comfortably, thereby avoiding the problem of putting children on the spot. This assumption is that there is no unique thought or action: if one person has had a thought or carried out an action, so have many others. What is the most unacceptable thought or action you can imagine? Even if you assume that it is thought or acted on by only one percent of the entire United States population, that one percent will include about two million people.

Knowing that fact does not mean you should condone all thoughts or acts. In an extreme situation, you might even want to prevent someone from telling you something that you sense you would be either legally or emotionally unable to handle. Even then you can help immeasurably by sharing that assumption, letting children know that many people have problems or worries they cannot share with parents, that many people use other resources (perhaps professionals) and find help, and that you, like many other parents, are willing to help them find such resources.

Other traps people get in and out of:

The trap: You told your children a fairy story about the stork. Now what do you do?

Getting out: Remind them of the Santa Claus myth and say, "Now you're old enough to know."

The trap: You got flustered once and said, "You're too young to understand." Now your child won't talk to you any more.

The out: Reopen the door. "Remember when I said you were too young? Now you're old enough; let's talk about it." Even if your child doesn't want to right that minute, he or she probably will soon, if not about that question, then another.

The trap: You got impatient when your child didn't understand, asked too many questions, or asked at the wrong time. You feel you were unfair, but now it's too late.

The out: Reopen the door. "You know, I was thinking about our conversation last week. I think I was unfair. . ."

Some of these things sound so obvious that you may wonder why on earth anyone would have any question about them. But it's amazing how often everyone— including the experts— overlook the obvious when under pressure.

The trap: You're on the spot with a question that is complicated, and you can't think how to answer. Maybe it's one that's causing your child a lot of anxiety or fear. The more you try to think, the blanker your mind gets, and the more frightened your child looks.

The out: "Boy, you've asked a tough one! I'm not stalling because I'm embarrassed or mad at you. I'm just having a hard time trying to figure out the best way to answer you. Just give me a minute to think about it, okay?"

That takes the heat off of both of you, and you can go ahead and think as long as you need to. Your child will be pleased that you consider his or her concerns worthy of real thought, no matter how anxious he or she is. You are being the model for the thoughtful parent that you hope your child will be some day.

In the end, it's often not the answer itself that counts, but the empathy you show, the attitude you impart, and the feelings that you share. Those are the things that will really be remembered. If your children want a textbook, they can eventually buy one. All they want from a parent or teacher is a reasonably knowledgeable, caring, understanding, and honest adult.

Worksheets:

The next few pages will give some situations that have happened to other people, with various ways they have been handled. Choose the way you think is most suitable, and then see how I might have handled them and why.

Before you begin, let's talk a minute about such worksheets. Many people find it difficult even in home questionnaires to resist checking the answer they think they are supposed to give, rather than the answer they really believe. Remember that this section is not to test you, but to help you.

The worksheets may be more helpful if you use them in this way: First check the answer you think I will give. Decide whether you agree or disagree with it, then go back and check the answer you think is best. Next, go back again and check what you would really be apt to do or say, and then compare notes with me. This will provide an instant check on whether or not I have made my point of view clear to you, and will enable you to answer more honestly.

The Situation:

You and your four year old are watching television. You suddenly realize that while watching, he or she is handling his or her genitals. You say or ask

a. "Stop that! bad boy/girl!"

b. "Do you have to go to the bathroom?" Or "Is your underwear too tight? Does something hurt you?"

c. "Don't do that."

d. "What are you doing? And why?"

e. "Hey, if you want to feel your penis/vagina, it's okay, but do it when you're alone. It's not polite in front of others."

f. Ignore it.

g. Find something else for him or her to hold.

My Answer:

For the first time or two, I'd choose *f.* "Ignore it." If it began happening more often, I'd pick *e* because it is a quick way of giving attitudes, ground rules for appropriate behavior and of defining what you're talking about without putting a child on a spot. If you use answer *d* it makes a child embarrassed, and he usually doesn't know what to say. Answer *b* can be checked out, but usually the child is having no problem at all and your message is very unclear. It's also confusing to hear, "Don't do that." Often children handle themselves so absentmindedly that they wouldn't know what you were talking about. You can use answer *g* once in a while but it won't stop a child from masturbating if masturbating is what he wants to do.

If open masturbation occurs repeatedly in what appears to be an uncontrolled or compulsive behavior, despite using my answers, you might suspect something else is going on like tension, boredom, fear, or anger. If it's a situational problem, that situation needs to be discussed. If it's general, you'd want to handle the masturbation the way you would any repeated inappropriate behavior, but you should get some counselling to help deal with more basic problems.

If you believe that masturbation is immoral, you can't use my answers at all. After all, you don't want to encourage immoral behavior, public or private. In that case you might have to use a more clearly defined *a* or *c*. But read the section on masturbation before you make a final decision.

The Situation:

Your five year old child of the opposite sex suddenly walks in and gets in the shower with you. You say

    a. "Get out of here!"

    b. "Please leave. You know this door was closed."

    c. "Go away, come back, and this time knock."

    d. "Hi," hand him or her the soap and start scrubbing.

My Answer:

It would depend on what had gone on before, and what I was trying to teach at the time. I'd use *d* for a door opener, or *b* or *c* to teach about privacy. If I was sure that it was merely the usual forgetting of house rules, like forgetting to close the screen door, I'd pick *b*, *c*, or even *a*.

The Situation:

You are a teacher of beginning reading. You have used the word "it," and are now going to go through the alphabet, putting letters in front of it to show how a new word is formed (b-it, c-it, f-it, etc.). When you reach "sh" and "t," some of the kids begin snickering. You

    a. Keep a straight face and go on.

    b. Rush over it quickly. ·

    c. Say, "Yes, that's a word, too. Know what it means? Let's stop and talk about it for a minute and see why you are laughing."

My Answer:

Again, it would depend on what was happening. For a door opener, I'd use *c*. For a clincher, I'd use *a*.

The Situation:

Your eleven or twelve year old tells you that a friend of hers "did the thing you do to have a baby." You say

    a. "You mean intercourse? That he put his penis in her vagina? What did she say about it? What do you think about it?"

    b. "That's terrible!"

    c. "Wow, that's pretty young. What do you think about it?"

    d. "Boy, they're starting young these days."

My Answer:

I'd pick *a*, *c* would be my second choice. I'd wonder why at that age she was not using the right term. By using answer *a*, I would give her information without embarrassing her in case she'd forgotten, while imparting an attitude of "it's all right to talk about it." At the same time, it would be a quick check on whether we were thinking along the same lines because some youngsters think that kissing makes babies.

The Situation:

Your thirteen year old has read a book that goes into graphic detail about intercourse and oral sex. You want to talk about it either because you consider the book obscene or feel that it might have engendered questions and perhaps fright. You have no idea what your child has done or knows about. You say or ask

a. "You're too young for that book!"

b. "That's a terrible book. It makes sex dirty and vulgar. Normal people don't do the things that book talks about."

c. "You know, books like that are okay if you take them for what they are—money makers for the authors and turn-on's for the readers. But they can give a lot of misinformation, and sometimes kids get the wrong idea of intercourse or sex in general. Maybe we should talk over some of the questions that you must be having."

d. "How did you happen to read it? Are the other kids reading it too? What do you think of it?" After you get a response, you say, "You know, a lot of people are rather shocked by it. And I would imagine that you might have mixed feelings about some of the things described, like where she puts his penis in her mouth. It might sound like fun, but then again it might sound pretty weird or frightening. Maybe we should talk about some of those things."

My Answer:

This is probably one of the many times when you are apt to find a discrepancy between your "right" answer and your "honest" one. Your first impulse, if you are being honest, might understandably be a panicky *a* or *b*. But if the teenager is interested enough to read the book, he or she is old enough to discuss it. Both *d* and *c* have useful parts to them, like getting the teenager to voice his or her own opinions, empathizing with possible feelings, and letting him or her know that those feelings are shared by others. I'd probably start out with the more general comments and questions of either one. But here comes the hard part. Staying "general" at first keeps you from launching into a discussion of something that the child may not have even read, much less worried about. But if he or she does not then ask specific questions, you may find yourself in a hole.

Jumping into the specifics of *d* might call for much mental throat clearing, because whether you consider oral sex immoral and obscene, or moral and fun, talking with teenagers about it can pose a problem. Behavior that seems all right to do, or read about or talk about in highly technical terms, can sound harsh, horrible and dirty when taken out of context and described. I would take the plunge and describe the behavior in question. There is a risk that it may be the one topic not read, but it's a slim chance. If you're having trouble getting the words out, you can be sure that your child is having even more trouble, and will never do so unless you take the first step. Unless you do take that step, your door opener may not work, and that book may become an important influence in your child's education.

Remember that in reading, the description will have been softened by the fact that it was in context. Also, since such subjects are hard to get into with no hook on which to hang a conversation, I don't get too upset about having a book like that around the house. It makes such a good door opener.

The Situation:

You're talking with your teenager, but she says scornfully, "I know all that stuff, I'm not a baby." You

a. Retire as gracefully as you can. If you feel defeated, you try not to show it.

b. Say, "Great, but the more you know in this area, the more there is to know. Asking questions or talking things over doesn't label anyone as dumb or babyish, now or in the future."

c. Say, "How do you know?"

d. Say, "Maybe you do, but I imagine it's more a case of being embarrassed, and we can get over that. And remember that your friends may give you wrong information. I sure hope you'll check out answers with me."

e. Say, "Gee, in that case I've been talking down to you, and that must be pretty annoying. Maybe part of the problem is that I don't really know what you've done or what you know, and you're a bit worried about telling me. I can't promise what my reactions will be, but why don't we take a chance on each other?"

My Answer:

I'd pick any answer but *c*, depending on the responses I was was getting, probably trying to work my way to *e*. But again, the answer that gets you furthest puts you in another hole. You've opened another door, but your child might be hesitant to walk through it. I might then even say, "Look, I don't mean to pry, and I'll understand if you don't want to talk about your private life. But I think I could help more if I knew where you were at. Can I just ask which of these things you've done: holding hands, kissing, petting, oral sex, having intercourse, etc.? Or if you don't want me to know, at least which of those things are you wondering about?"

If that doesn't open things up, you may just need to keep the door open, and perhaps provide a book so that he or she gets good information from someone, even if it isn't you.

The Situation:

You got a direct answer, now you almost wish you hadn't asked. You don't want your child to regret her honesty, but you have mixed feelings; pride and relief at the candor, but also worry, fear, anger. You

a. Play it cool and non-judgmental.

b. Explode. That's you and you're honest.

c. Share your mixed emotions, your concerns. You point out her responsibilities, and thank her for playing it straight with you. Maybe you leave the door open for the future by saying that you probably both have mixed feelings at this point, and should take time out to think over the things you've discussed; but now at least you have some idea of the kinds of things she will probably want to talk over one of these days.

My Answer:

Again, your probable answer of *c* (mine, also) may not agree with your honest answer. Just remember that you can always reopen the subject merely by saying, "You know, I gave last night's talk a lot of thought. I didn't think I'd be so shockable, but now that I'm more together, let's talk. I'd like you to know. . . . ."

The Situation:

You received a confidence from your spouse about your child's petting, with permission to talk it over with the child. You

a. Do not mention it to the child.

b. Refer to it indirectly. ("I know what you want the car for," or "Going out with John? No necking tonight!")

    c. Say, "Dad told me of your talk and I want you to know I firmly disapprove!"

    d. Say, "Mom told me; I want you to know that we realize how much courage it took to tell us, and we appreciate it. But I think there are some things we'd better talk about."

My Answer:

I'd pick *d*. Answer *a* makes everyone walk on eggs wondering who knows and what and the child builds up fear. *B* or *c* can close doors and cut off communication not only with you, but with the original confidante.

The Situation:

You want to discuss birth control, but you're not sure how to start. You

    a. Say, "Now that you're getting older, we'd better start talking about birth control. Any time you need to or want to, feel free. And if you'd like to talk now, fine!"

    b. Mention this book, a conversation with someone else, or ask your daughter's or son's opinions of birth control and when facts should be given.

    c. Say, "When you start having intercourse, you'd better check with me."

My Answer:

I'd pick *a* or *b*. Since this is a sensitive subject that many parents have trouble with, let's follow it through a potential problem or two. What if your child says, "I don't need to know! Don't you trust me?" Do you answer

    a. "Frankly, no."

    b. "It's not a question of trusting—I just know that from now on, you'll have to be making decisions about pre-marital intercourse. Much as I want you to be able to talk to me, I realize you may not wish to or be able to at the time; but you'll need the information. I'd rather give you the facts before you need them than after."

    c. "Well, I am wondering what's happening, and would like to have a talk in order to be of help. But I'm not accusing you of anything—I just think you're old enough to have the information you need. It's only fair."

You might need to choose *a*, but it's a door slammer. Answer *b* or *c* could get you farther. If nothing helps, you again might use a book as your only alternative. You might want to give out a book as a clincher, with a reminder that the doctor is the best authority on choosing birth control methods.

The Situation:

Your eighteen-year old daughter tells you she is planning to live with her boyfriend; she wants to be honest with you, but wants your blessing (not permission). You

   a. Ask what they see as advantages and disadvantages, potential problems, and how they plan to handle those problems. You give your opinion, but no matter what it is, you also give your blessing.

   b. You try to talk them out of it.

   c. You tell her she is no longer welcome in your house.

My Answer:

I'd pick *a*, recognizing that my parental concern might unintentionally sneak in a bit of *b*. I would avoid *c* like the plague. But that's me. I saw one mother reduced to tears in a role playing session when she chose *c*, and was accused of being a terrible mother. I hardly think that was a fair accusation. We all have some point at which we draw a line regarding morality, and even our children cannot cross that line without thinking about the consequences. Make sure, however, that this line is really worth the added agony that will ensue for everyone.

The Situation:

You'd like your parents to share in the sexual revolution, but they have never talked about sex, and you don't want to invade their privacy.

   a. You mention an article or conversation about sex and the older person, and ask your parent's opinion about it.

   b. You mention an upcoming workshop on sex and the older person (widow, etc.) that you think might be of interest.

   c. You mention changes in your life, wonder if the same was true for them. If they get huffy or embarrassed, you apologize, say you didn't mean to pry, you just thought it might be useful to talk about it.

   d. When your teenager pulls a *faux pas* in front of them (example: "Why doesn't Mrs. Jones act her age?" or

"Who'd look at him? He's ancient!" or "My teacher probably never heard of sex, she's an old maid."), you laugh
and say, "Who says you have to be young to enjoy sex?
I know people who have more fun at eighty than they
had at eighteen, and I sure hope to, myself.

My Answer:

Any answer might be fine, depending upon the situation.
You have provided information in the last one, to both parent and
child, without invading privacy. If your parent looks embarrassed,
you can always apologize later in private.

The Situation: ·

You disapprove of the fact that your child is having intercourse. Aside from your moral concerns, you worry that negative
experiences now will prevent a happy sexual relationship later on
in life. You

a. Tell him or her exactly that.
b. Choose *a*, adding that while you don't approve of his or
    her decision, you know that achieving a happy, loving re-
    lationship is not always easy, and that you will still want
    to offer help with any questions or problems he or she
    may have.
c. Say, "It's your decision, but don't ask me to help you
    make things any easier."

My Answer:

I'd take *a* and *b*. I might even joke about the fact that we'd
both have to swallow hard before asking or answering the first
questions.

You might want to try out some of these questions using different ages, sexes and behaviors. These answers have pointed out
the fact that there are very few simple answers, especially for some
of the complicated issues during adolescence and they are useful
only as guides for your thinking.

The situations discussed in this chapter have been primarily
problems in communications. The subject matter they presented
is much more complex. I suggest that after you have read the
chapters on these issues you then review these problems and see if
your reactions have been changed.

Homework:

Paper answers tend to be stilted, and imaginary conversations always go the way you want them to. Neither really gives you practice in dealing with the give and take of a real conversation. For this reason, role playing (acting out a scene with another person) is often more useful. You can modify the rules to fit your needs.

Take any example in the book or make one up. The typical role playing situation consists of three people: one person takes the role of the child, one the role of the parent, and one the role of the observer. Each person is given the bare essentials of his character and the scene, and the situation is then acted out, each actor ad libbing and playing it as if he or she were really that person in that situation. After a specified time, the action stops, the observer shares his or her observations, and the actors discuss their own inner reactions and their feelings about their partner. It goes around three times, so that each person has a chance to be a parent, a child, and an observer.

A few ground rules must be observed: "parents" must be the best parents they know how to be, "children" the best children that they can be. Nobody is allowed to say later that he deliberately played the sullen adolescent or the nasty parent. Each person plays the sex he or she is in real life (unless there is a special reason to change the rules). Sometimes role playing becomes hilarious; while a sense of humor is essential, laughing should be held to a minimum, or nobody will really be able to get into the part. While really honest evaluations are the main objective, this strictly excludes cruel, personal putdowns. Remember the mother who was reduced to tears because somebody broke that rule.

Role playing can be done with friends, students, adults or children or a combination. Three different situations can give a wider variety of skills to practice, while the same situation each time gives people the chance to benefit from past mistakes. While role playing is sometimes hard work, and people often feel awkward and embarrassed at first, it helps in developing warmth and empathy, communication skills, and self-awareness. Once it gets going, it usually is a lot of fun.

CHAPTER SIX

COMMON LITTLE—AND NOT SO LITTLE—
PROBLEMS IN DAILY LIVING

One of the hardest things about being a parent is the constant decision making. There are a certain number of very big decisions about very big problems, and these can be agonizing. But it is probably the minor every day decisions, so quickly made that we don't even term them problems, that become so wearing: Should I let Tommy have a snack before supper? Does Jane's behavior merit punishment? Should I let Jimmy watch a monster movie?

The same is true in the area of sex: There may be big problems, such as what to do if a child has been molested or becomes pregnant, that cause a great deal of anguish. But it is the little decisions—should I lock the door?—is the deadline I set reasonable?—and should we let them see an R-rated movie? that send parents to the medicine cabinet for tranquilizers.

It is impossible to cover all the questions that come up, but here are the ones that I am either asked most often or that seem to be of most concern.

Is nudity harmful? How much should be allowed in the home? At what age should children be prevented from going around nude or from seeing their parents undressed?

There is nothing harmful in nudity, given a certain amount of moderation. How much, or even if, really depends on an individual family. I think that a little nudity is useful. I don't even worry about it if my teenagers, who are usually even more embarrassed than I, catch me once in a while. Teenagers need to know how people look as they get older.

But I also think that children should be taught early to respect privacy. Closed doors should be honored by everyone, child and adult alike. My husband and I, however, have seldom locked or permitted locking doors, partly for safety reasons and partly to emphasize that "knocking" not "locking" is the rule in our house. This means that we have had some occasional embarrassing moments, but I far prefer them to the implications of locked doors, especially with small children who may become frightened.

If parents are constantly parading around nude, it can be, but is not necessarily, overstimulating or seductive to the occasional child, particularly as he or she begins to reach puberty. Also, children may worry about bringing friends home to meet undressed parents.

Childhood nudity will depend on the situation and the culture. The problem often takes care of itself; children themselves become shy at certain stages. My son, for instance, suddenly decided at the age of four that he must not be seen in his underwear. No power on earth could make him try on trousers in a store aisle, even though ten other four year olds were in the same aisle, trying on trousers with their underwear showing. Some children will swim nude at a public beach with no qualms until they are seven or eight. On the other hand, a two year old watching her older sister with a two-piece bathing suit, may insist on wearing the same thing.

Teenagers, especially between the ages of ten and fourteen, are the most easily embarrassed people in the world, and hence they usually determine the stopping time for nudity. Many a parent has complained to me, "We never had hangups or closed doors, so why are our kids suddenly so embarrassed about everything? What did we do wrong?" They had probably done nothing wrong. Their children were probably just coping with new feelings and body changes, and were very unsure of themselves. Adults often forget how embarrassing that stage of development can be to the person going through it.

Probably most children unintentionally see other family members nude at times no matter how carefully one tries to prevent it. Treated casually, nudity will be less exciting or upsetting to all concerned.

When should children stop being bathed by or sleeping with parents of the opposite sex?

Again this question usually takes care of itself. Parents often find bathing a chore they are glad to be rid of as soon as children can manage it by themselves. By the time they are seven or eight years old they have outgrown the cuddliness that makes them acceptable in beds. Even if the parents don't mind, children themselves become shy or resent being babied. There is no exact point for discontinuing either behavior and any age I set is arbitrary, useful only as a general guideline. It becomes difficult to say "Yesterday you could do these things but today you can't," so here are some general guidelines.

For sleeping arrangements, the earlier a child can be in its own room the better, starting the day the infant is brought home from the hospital. Not only does this preserve parental sanity, it also avoids the need for changes that might be upsetting to a child later on. Yet if financial problems necessitate a child sleeping with parents past the age of six or seven, it need not be a matter of great concern. Occasional crawling into bed with a parent is fun and beneficial to children under the age of six, and a period of stress, for example a nightmare, a parent's absence or death, may make such a request reasonable even after that. It should not be allowed to develop into a habit that will interfere with parental privacy or with the child's development of independence. One can be firm and remain sensitive to a particular child at a particular time. One child, for example, may need a firm rule like "I sleep in my bed and you sleep in yours." Another may need an explanation or reassurance that the change in rules is not rejection, but a tribute to growing up, with parental affection given in more adult ways.

The guidelines for bathing are even less clear, since it partly depends on age and partly on a child's ability to bathe alone. Children are often able to accomplish this by the time they are three or four; after the age of seven or eight, the question usually arises only if a child is handicapped, temporarily hurt or ill. If your intuition fails, I'd suggest that both practices be tapered off and discontinued at least by the age of nine or ten and certainly by the time a child shows the beginning signs of pubescence. Mainly these guidelines are to establish 'growing up' in the child's mind, but they will also hold potential unwanted sexual stimulation to a minimum.

Tips:

Sometimes a young child will have an erection or comment about it tickling when a parent washes the genitals. This is a natural occurrence, meaning only that a child has experienced pleasant sensations usually associated with that part of the body. It is best handled casually. One mother, for instance, laughed when this happened, saying, "It feels good, doesn't it!" She neither lingered nor rushed over the genital area, and it assumed no importance of any kind. If it happens often with a child over six or seven, that might be a clue that it's time to let the child bathe alone.

Sometimes it's impossible for a parent of the same sex to take over during illness. For an older child who, say, has been hurt and needs help in the tub, some discretion and tact will be needed, plus some empathy. It is possible to train one's self to "not see." It will be reassuring to the child to know that a parent is both willing and able to do that; and also it will provide a model for a child who unintentionally catches a parent undressed.

What should you do if your child pops in on you while you're having intercourse?

It is sad but true that this happens every so often. Come to think of it, I'm not sure that it's all that sad, though it sure can put a damper on things. What you do will depend on you, the child, the age, and the situation. You might say, "The door is closed, that means we want privacy. Go away!" You might say, "Next time, please knock! You know the rule!" If you can get away with it, you might just pretend you weren't really doing anything anyhow.

If children ask what you're doing, seem scared (young children often are), hang around or "pop in" so often that you suspect they're coming in accidentally on purpose, you might explain that you were "making love." Tell them that you like privacy, and they should come back later. Very young children probably won't think to ask what "making love" means, but if they are old enough to think of the question, they are old enough to deserve an honest answer. You don't, however, have to give it to them at that moment. The only thing you need to do, if a young child looks frightened, is to provide reassurance that everything is all right. If you haven't yet talked about intercourse, you might use that as your door opener at the first convenient moment afterward. Even if you have explained once, you might refer back to your past talk and explain again if necessary.

What do you do if your children sleep in the same room or the walls are paper thin?

Close living quarters are part of life for a good many families. If you can't do anything about it, relax and stop worrying. However, remember that small children may not know how to interpret the strange signs and sounds, and sometimes think their parents are having a fight, or that someone is getting hurt. So you might casually comment some day, "Sometimes you may hear us making funny sounds or see us moving around in bed a lot. We're just loving each other in a special way called having intercourse, and it makes us feel good. Okay?"

Children will probably say, "Okay" and not think about it. If they haven't ever noticed what you've been doing, they will think you're kind of crazy, but most kids think adults are crazy anyway. If they have noticed, they'll probably be relieved. Of course you fit your explanation to your child. Again, it'll be easier if you have already talked about intercourse, and if you haven't, that can be your door opener.

What do you do when your teenagers stay up later than you or you get the urge during the day when they are around?

Many parents expect to find things easier when the children get older, and then find that having a sophisticated teenager around makes them more uncomfortable than ever about their sexual life. Trying to get them to bed early is fine, but it's usually a losing battle.

Have fun! It's about time your teenagers, or even your "in-betweeners", realized that people over thirty—including not only parents in general, but pot-bellied, grey-haired ones too—are sexual beings. The same thing applies to daytime activity, assuming you're using a certain amount of moderation. By then you should have talked with your children enough so that you can say, "We want to be alone for a little while," and they will get the idea. Slightly younger children may be less sensitive. There's nothing wrong with laying it on the line.

Self control is fine, but sometimes love in the afternoon is a badly needed treat for any marriage. Don't be so embarrassed! You're not committing a crime! You are, in fact, giving some beautiful sex education by treating your sexuality as a warm and loving relationship that requires privacy, but not secrecy.

Once when our children were about eleven, we got the urge on a beautiful Saturday afternoon. We had never permitted ourselves such luxuries before, but we sent them off to a basketball game, and of course, for the first time in their lives, they did not want to go. Then a visitor appeared, and by the time he had left, the children had returned. We forced them to go out to play, but later, while we were still lounging sleepily in bed, our son suddenly walked in. There was nothing we could do—we were caught! We chatted with him, trying to appear casual, until he said, "Hey! What are you doing in bed at this time of day? What are you doing undressed? Hey, you weren't — were you — making love? Is that why you were trying to get rid of us?" We nodded, feeling very foolish. He looked a bit flustered for a moment, then burst out laughing. "Whew!" he said. "Why didn't you just say that's what you wanted to do? We thought you were mad at us!"

Well, as we say at our house, nobody's perfect. But that taught us to have more faith in the principle we had known but perhaps had not fully believed—that honesty is much less frightening to children than secrecy. Despite the embarrassment, we were certainly glad that our decision to not lock the door had at least afforded an opportunity for them to learn that we were not "mad" at them.

Should boys be taught about sex by men and girls be taught by women?

Many parents will say quickly, "Go ask your father" or "Go ask your mother" when a child of the opposite sex asks a question or will tell each other, "I think it's time you had a talk with John or Jane." This is both a door closer and poor modeling behavior which contradicts what you supposedly are trying to teach: which is, that it is possible to talk rationally and comfortably about sex, with the opposite sex.

"Modeling," by the way, is a term I use often. It merely means that we all learn by example, hence the behavior that you use acts as a "model" for your children. They may unconsciously copy it, and derive attitudes from it. If you say one thing and do another, your modeling will outweigh what you say. So the best model for communication between the sexes is for the parent or teacher to answer whatever is asked when it is asked, or deal with whatever situation has arisen, no matter what the sex of the child in question.

Of course sometimes you may not be able to answer a question, you may want a child to know the other sex's viewpoint, you may want someone to back you up, or you may want to encourage communication with someone of the opposite sex. But, "Why don't you see how Dad feels about it, now that you know how I feel," or "Mom may be able to explain better than I have, let's ask her," is a lot different than, "Go ask your father or mother."

At certain stages, often in the early teens, children themselves may feel much more comfortable with an adult of their sex, and the closeness of man-man or woman-woman talk helps them to identify with the strengths of that adult. You may even have to encourage a child to talk with the other parent.

Finally, I think there are times when talking about sex is a family affair, times when it is a man to man or woman to woman affair, and times when it is a man-woman affair. Exclusion of any of the three is limiting. If you are a single parent, you will need to find ways to provide an opportunity for discussion with someone of the other sex.

What kinds of words should be used? Baby words? Euphemisms? Scientific terms? Four-letter words?

Our society is a marvellous study in confusing contradictions when it comes to the language of sex. On the one hand we go to any lengths to avoid using correct terms, and on the other hand, we insist on such long, complicated terminology that everything sounds like a disease. Often we talk about sex by not talking about it. "Mary and John were. . . .you know." Confusing as the communication is, it is precise enough to allow off-color jokes to be told on television and immediately understood, using no reference to sex at all. No matter what words we use, we manage to convey the idea that sex is too "bad" to be discussed freely.

What words to use will depend on what is understandable and acceptable according to the particular age, locale, and culture. If you're teaching children in Hawaii, as I am, it seems pointless to use terms that only a New Yorker would understand; conversely, many Hawaiian terms would be meaningless to New Yorkers. Scientific words are fine, but if you talk about other parts of your body, you use the simplest words possible in every day conversation: jaw instead of mandible, leg instead of femur. Why should it be so different in sex?

The four letter words sound vulgar only because we have made them so. Nevertheless, even little children can learn proper terms, and the earlier you start, the better. They should know a variety of terms and the differences. For example, we use a variety of words for anger (mad, sore, disgusted) and happiness (joy, pleasure), and children learn easily enough which words fit which situation. They can do the same for sexual words.

Of course you might not want your four year old going around saying "fuck"—or your twelve year old—or even your twenty-one year old. But twenty-one year olds are able to tell when such words are appropriate; four or twelve year olds may not be. So it's probably better not to use such words around your youngster too much (you needn't be upset if one pops out once in a while and your child hears it). If you do allow such words in your household, you'd better make it clear that while you permit them, Aunt Bertha, Teacher, or their best friend's mother might not be so accepting.

Some authorities disagree, but I think that euphemisms such as "making love" are all right. If the child also knows the correct terms and what the euphemisms imply, they're easier and sound nicer than the antiseptic "sexual intercourse." Many children are confused by "sleeping with," and I myself remember nearly ending up in a heap of trouble as a teenager—a pretty naive one, I must admit—when I agreed to let a date "make love" to me. I didn't learn until after I'd slapped his surprised face and been scared silly, what I'd given permission for. I'd thought "making love" meant kissing. Fortunately, my date was no rapist, realized I had misunderstood, and apologized. Another teenager might not have been so lucky.

I also know a retarded teenager who became hysterical when a male swimming instructor gave her physical support while teaching her to float. It turned out that she had been told by her mother never to let a man "touch" her, or she would get pregnant. Mama knew what she meant by that term, but the daughter took it literally.

Tip:

Terms vary from locale to locale, and generation to generation. Be sure that you and the child with whom you are talking understand your terms; for example, "making out" can mean kissing, petting, or intercourse, depending upon the person, the age, or the city. If you pussy-foot around in defining terms, you can ruin a parent-child relationship through miscommunication or give a wrong diagnosis if you are a doctor or therapist.

The main thing to remember is that anything you can do to enhance communication is appropriate, providing you are not unduly delaying or avoiding words that a child needs to know. You can be correct or tactful but if a child doesn't understand you, what good does it do?

I once knew a teacher who couldn't understand why one of the smarter and more "experienced" boys in her adolescent sex education class suddenly seemed so embarrassed and was acting so unintelligently. Finally, during a private talk with him, he said angrily, "Naw, I ain't embarrassed. I'll talk about sex, but not if you use all those long nutty words. Talk to me in words I understand!" She continued to teach correct terminology; but when she also used his language, she found that he knew more than either of them had realized. He stopped feeling so dumb, and hence became less embarrassed. Only then did they get down to the nitty gritty of real problems with which he was struggling.

Here is some homework you can do:

Having trouble spitting out some of those words? Then practice. Say them in front of a mirror while alone, with your spouse, or with friends willing to practice with you. Look up definitions for words you don't know, and talk over what each word implies. In this exercise try using both correct terminology and common street words.

Knowing the common or four letter words and being able to say them does not mean you have to, should, or would ever want to use them. But if the occasion ever arises when they're useful, it will be easier. It will help you avoid rising to the bait when children try to shock you, as they inevitably do sooner or later.

An eleven year old, after being told that such words were permitted occasionally in their household, once announced at the dinner table that he'd be glad when he got old enough to fuck girls. There was a heavy silence while the mother struggled with her feelings, and the boy waited expectantly to see what would happen. The mother tried not to act shocked, but finally explained her feelings about that word—at least the way in which he was using it—and suggested that until he had had enough experience to know where and when it could be used without offending anyone, she'd rather he not use it. Four years later, she reports that she has never heard him use it since.

Tip:

If you are a teacher, a professional or helping out in some community program, don't assume that just because a parent or child is from a different social or cultural background, he or she will not understand correct terms or will enjoy four letter ones. The use of words, like anything else, requires sensitivity to the needs and values of the particular person with whom you are dealing.

What should you do if a child wants to tell you dirty jokes?

Many parents today are taken quite by surprise when their

children decide to tell them dirty jokes. Such a thing would have been unthinkable with their own parents, and they are quite uncertain what their attitude should be. I know, this happened with me, but I am very glad now that our son told his first joke to us. It gave him a chance to try out and learn what is funny and what isn't, just as he'd done earlier when he'd pulled out the whole Joe Miller joke book. By our reactions, non-reactions, and occasional explanations, he learned something about our values, and we were able to help him establish to whom his behavior would be acceptable. Of course that meant he eventually stopped telling us jokes and words that I'm sure he still told the gang. I'm also sure that he won't be in much danger of offending people now, that he'll choose both jokes and words according to the people he's with, and that he will differentiate between "dirty" jokes and casual, joking humor about sex. Actually, he announced after a very short trial period that he was embarrassed telling jokes to his mother, and accordingly, quickly stopped doing it.

Pre-adolescent jokes, by the way, are usually connected with excretory functions, early adolescent jokes with the size of genitals and breasts, and only later do they deal with intercourse or oral sex. They have the useful function of helping kids cope with worries about themselves and their changing bodies and social skills, in the same way that jokes about marriage often help parents cope with marital frustrations. Told in moderation, they are usually nothing to worry about.

Interestingly enough, we seem to have a double standard that considers it all right for adults to tell dirty jokes, but not for children or adolescents to do so. That hardly makes much sense. So if you object to hearing kids tell dirty stories, be consistent with your modeling. I actually see nothing wrong with occasional casual talk and humor about sex while children are around; I believe it gives a more human concept of sex.

I often note that adults will stop dead if children, including teenagers, walk in while they are telling a dirty joke or even just talking about sex, flounder around trying to change the subject, or say significantly to their companions, "I'll tell you later!" in a stage whisper that can be heard across the room. They are fooling no one but themselves. What they are doing is telling children that talking about sex is dirty but exciting behavior, reserved for a special exclusive club which they will certainly want to join.

In most instances, it would probably be better to keep right on going, finish the joke or the sentence smoothly, and then switch to another subject if it seems appropriate. Children will pay less attention to a joke they do not understand, and if old enough to understand, they should either be allowed to hear it or told honestly that they have walked into a private conversation and should come back later.

How should you react to "doctor" games or a little boy pulling down a little girl's panties?

I don't think parents or teachers need get too upset about children exploring each others' bodies, as long as the children are of approximately the same age, size and mental ability, and as long as it occurs in moderation and in appropriate private situations with the consent of both children. Of course you'll want to talk about "appropriate" behavior, with the ground rules that apply to most behavior. Certainly such games are not appropriate on the schoolgrounds or in any other public place. If they are happening continually with certain children, one might suspect that these children are looking for information that should be given in other ways, or showing problems that should receive attention.

Most children explore occasionally to compare their bodies with those of others. They may even simulate intercourse, the way they simulate other aspects of playing house. Sometimes children report and complain about having their underwear pulled down, because they sense that adults will disapprove. The children feel a bit guilty, yet they will go on allowing it even if told they shouldn't. You might let them know that curiosity is natural, but that they should stop it if they want to. The basic ground rules you want to establish are that older children should not be doing this with younger children, and stronger children should not force themselves on weaker children. If that happens, of course you have to intervene. Sometimes, however, it's hard to know when it's been forced; you stand a better chance of determining that if you have not deliberately made a child feel guilty about exploration.

Five year olds don't get pregnant, venereal disease, or bad reputations from playing games; twelve year olds may. The age at which to stop exploration or sex play is an unanswerable question, for it will depend on the individual. The chances are that no matter what you say or do, some of it will take place throughout life. The only question will be how much guilt and responsibility will accompany it, and the older children get, the more they need to know about their responsibility and the consequences of their actions.

How do you prevent impulsive behavior?

This question goes back to that worry about "planting" ideas in a child's mind and the fear that once an idea has been planted, a child will commit some unacceptable sexual act. There's no way for adults to prevent sexual exploration, but there is a technique used by therapists with patients who they fear may misinterpret their "understanding" or who may act impulsively out of anger. Again basically common sense, it can be used effectively by parents and teachers. It's called "anticipating with"; it means that if you anticipate that children might interpret your discussion as "permission," you can anticipate out loud, including the concern that you have and using the *many people* concept.

For example: "You know, sometimes children go home and try out some of the words we use in class on their parents. I know it's fun to shock people, but don't do it!" "It occurs to me that because we talk a lot about intercourse before marriage, you might feel we're giving you permission to go ahead. We're not —in fact we'd rather you wouldn't." "You know, many teenagers say they won't have sex in order to please their parents. But then at some point when the parents have hurt them or angered them in some way, they have sex just to hurt back. So make sure that what you do is based on a real decision about what is best for you." Note that the *many people* principle allows for discussion without accusing children of crimes they have not committed.

What To Tell Your Children About Child Molesters

Up until now we've been talking about common everyday matters. But many parents and teachers are concerned about a less common but potentially more serious concern—child molestation. At first glance this might seem a fairly simple subject to deal with. Most people, for example, warn children early in life not to accept candy from or go away with strangers. But having said that, they are often unsure about what to say next. Here are some problems people have brought to my attention:

"I warned my child not to accept candy from a stranger. She asked me why and I said, 'Because some people are bad and might try to hurt you.' Again she asked 'Why?' and 'What would they do?' and I was stuck. How could I talk about things like that with a four year old?"

"I'd planned to treat the subject of intercourse as a warm and loving relationship. But my child's first question was, 'What's rape?'"

"My ten year old came home from school all upset. Her teacher had warned the class about molesters and told them about horrible things that could happen to them if they spoke to strangers. Now she's afraid of all strangers. How do we deal with that?"

"I want my teenagers to think of sex—especially intercourse—as beautiful. How do I do that and still warn them about danger?"

Part of the problem for parents is that the subject so often comes up without giving them time to think through such basic issues as what specific information do I want to give my child? What am I myself most concerned about? How do I reconcile seemingly conflicting ideas like "sex is good" versus "sex is bad"? It's helpful, then, to think ahead and to clarify in your own mind your specific concerns. When they take time to think about it, the parents who talk to me usually name these concerns:

I am worried about violent physical abuse—that my child will be bruised, beaten, raped, or even murdered.

I worry that my child will become pregnant or contract a venereal disease.

I am afraid that my child will receive emotional scars.

These worries are valid; such possibilities do exist, and we all want to protect children from such dangers. Often, however, adults are overly worried and communicate excessive fear to children, because they either lack information or have misinformation about molestation. So before we go any further, here are some facts you should know about molesters, the nature of molestation, and the effects upon children.

Just what is molestation and how common is it?

Leroy Schultz, a social worker who has dealt extensively with problems of sexual abuse, points out that it is extremely difficult to obtain reliable information on the incidence of child molestation. This is because many situations go unreported. Also, he notes, it is because our society has not really defined what the term means. The legal definition varies from state to state. If it is difficult for the law to define the term, it is even more difficult for parents, who want their children to be friendly and approachable, and who also want adults to be friendly to their children. It becomes hard to define where appropriate displays of friendship or affection end and molestation begins. Misinterpretations of affectionate behavior have resulted in such injustices as teachers being accused of molestation merely because they put their arms around a child following a playground accident.

We often think of molestation in terms of violence, and certainly it does occur. The most common forms of offenses, however, are exhibitionism, general caressing and fondling, or sometimes specific stroking of the genitals. Schultz cites various studies showing that ninety percent of the offences do not involve violence or force. Exhibitionists are usually seeking to shock, not engage in a sexual act. With caressing and fondling, often the adult intends to show affection, and the child perceives the behavior as affectionate rather than sexual, with coercion neither needed nor used. Attempts at intercourse are far less frequent, and even they do not necessarily include violence.

How can you spot a potential child molester?

When talking about child molesters, the image often comes to mind of a dirty old man who skulks around schoolyards, lures children with candy, takes them to a secluded place, and rapes or kills them. While of course there are such people, the fact is (and it may not be all that reassuring to you) that most child molesters are neither "dirty old men" nor strangers. They are, according to many researchers, more apt to be in their twenties or thirties. Furthermore, they are apt to be people whom the child knows well, such as neighbors, friends of the family, or close relatives. Another myth refuted by research is that molesters are "oversexed"—actually the reverse is true. The child molester is more often a person so fearful of sexual relationships or uncertain of his or her own sexual abilities that he or she turns to children precisely because they give affection without having high sexual "performance" demands.

What are the effects of molestation upon children?

The effects, of course, will depend on the child and the situation. As Schultz points out, there may be no trauma at all, or there may be very severe emotional damage. Generally, his conclusions, based on various studies, are that probably less than five to ten percent of all child sex victims suffer physical damage or disease, and of those who do, the physical symptoms can often be treated quickly and successfully. Where no force or violence was used, most of the children studied were engaging in affection-seeking behavior and did not perceive the offense at the time as traumatic. Most sexual assaults do not affect the child's personality development negatively, particularly when neither violence nor subsequent court appearance is involved. Guilt in sex victims is fairly absent, but may be engendered by parents, courts, social services and the community after the fact. Adequate sex education that includes important aspects of sexuality and potential victimization, whether given by the family, church, school, or other social organization, may reduce the possibility of a child becoming a victim.

What does all this information mean to you in terms of how you will talk with children? It means that instead of worrying about specific people who might "look suspicious," you will need to think about specific behaviors, giving children guidelines for their own behavior, for evaluating the behavior of adults, and determining what is appropriate or inappropriate adult behavior in different situations. You will want to think through whether you regard a specific behavior as a worry and if so, why? For example, if an adult plays with a child's genitals, causing no particular harm, would that concern you because you are fearful that it might lead to intercourse or rape? Because it is "sinful?" Because it is an adult taking unfair advantage of a child? Even if no other reason exists, you might find it offensive because it seems inappropriate for adults to engage in sexual behaviors with children.

This information will also be useful to you in helping your children recognize their own rights. Schultz notes that children are reared in such a way that they cannot refuse adults. They are taught to be obedient, and to accept all forms of adult affection such as being hugged, patted, picked up, squeezed, and kissed. Children hence have little experience in saying no to an adult, in trusting their own reactions, or in resisting the promise of rewards. Furthermore, he points out the incongruity of keeping children uninformed about sexual matters and then wondering why they are so vulnerable to sexual advances. Even recognizing that they may not have the physical strength to resist adult demands, you can help children by letting them know that "obedience" has its limits, and they have the right to refuse.

You may say this does not actually tell you what to say to children, and there's no getting around it—there are no pat ways or answers for the questions raised by parents earlier. If you're thinking along these lines, however , you will be much more apt to give clear behavioral ground rules with understandable reasons, and you will cause less excessive fright and guilt than many parents do. For example, it may indeed be frightening—or even unbelievable—for a child to be told not to accept candy from a stranger because he or she might get hurt, or even because the adult might rape. You might add to your first explanation of intercourse—and here is yet another reason for giving that explanation as early as possible—a simple "By the way, intercourse is something only for adults; it's unfair for grown-ups to make children have intercourse with them, and if any adult tries, you should say 'No' and tell me about it." Such an approach should not be terribly frightening, but it will be clear.

Here are some other possible ground rules for children. Don't let any adult undress you unless it's for a good reason, like getting you ready for bed or the doctor needing to examine you. Don't let any adult show you his or her genitals or ask you to show yours. Don't let adults kiss you on the mouth, or lick you, play with your genitals or ask you to play with theirs. Those rules hold for all adults, including members of the family. You as a parent will decide on the particular behaviors, and the reasons you give. Again, there is always the old standby—that sexual behavior is for people of the same ages, and grownups are not the same age as children. You can always add that anyone who would be that unfair to children might also be so "mixed up" or whatever term you choose to use, that they might even hurt somebody, either by accident or on purpose.

There are ground rules for preventing adults from having the opportunity for such behavior. You can tell your child not to wander off with adults, without parental permission, even if candy is offered, or to accept rides with strangers. The reason you give your child is simple: While most people are nice and only want to be friendly, there are some people who are so mixed up inside that they use rides and candy as a way of getting children alone, and who then might hurt them sexually or otherwise. You might want to give the child ways of avoiding letting an adult know he or she is alone at home. You might rehearse telephone conversations or what the child might say to someone who knocks at the door. You can also teach children both by your words and your modeling that kissing and hugging are not for just anyone. Such behavior is reserved for people whom one knows well and of whom one is especially fond. This will be particularly important if you are dealing with a retarded child.

It's also important for a child to know what to do if a potentially dangerous situation occurs. For example, you might say that if an adult does try to undress him or her, the child should say "no" firmly, ask to go home, and if not allowed to, do anything possible to attract help or get away. An exhibitionist will be discouraged by being ignored, since he is really trying to shock, not hurt. Still, a child should guard against the unexpected, leave the scene quickly, find another adult and be accompanied home if at all possible.

This all sounds like strong, frightening stuff; but remember that you will not be giving it all at once, that you will be choosing words and details according to the child's age and the situation, and that your tone and attitude can prevent it from being frightening. While there are no recipes to give, there are at least some guidelines and tips to help you:

1. A big lecture is unnecessary and sets up sexuality as dangerous. Far better is the use of serendipity and door openers, which allows you to give information in bits and pieces as appropriate, and in context.

2. Warning about the dangers of sex is no different than warning about other dangers. For example, you teach children how to avoid being hit by a car, without ever implying that cars are bad, or that all drivers are out to hurt them. You can make such distinctions about sex too.

3. The possibility of sexual abuse is only one of several reasons for the ground rules you list—neither more nor less important than the other reasons. For example, children should not go away without your permission because they might get lost, the adult might forget to bring them back, or because you will be

worried. Slipped in with those other reasons, sexuality is just one more part of the life with which a child must learn to cope.

4. Try to be as explicit as possible, with directions and terms which are as simple as possible. You do not have to give every detail each time—much will depend on what you have said before.

5. You can be explicit without frightening the child. Words are not frightening. The way in which you use them is what makes the difference.

One parent reported this incident with an unusually verbal two and a half year old girl. The child had been instigating "doctor games" in her nursery school, at one time calling out from the playhouse, "Who wants to come and play doctor with me?" The teacher had said calmly but firmly, "Nobody, Barbie. We don't play those games in school!" Later while in the shower, Barbie asked her father if he would play doctor with her. Told no, she asked why not—her friends liked to. She again was told firmly, "Because adults do not play such games with children!" The parents also began to realize that their daughter was looking for information far earlier than they had expected her to, and began to provide other ways to satisfy curiosity than by body exploration. But these answers neither frightened her nor stirred up excessive guilt—they merely gave clear ground rules for appropriate behavior on the part of both children and adults.

Tip:

Not all "doctor" games include sexual activity. If your child should play doctor, be sure you know what that involves, or you may become needlessly concerned and provide inappropriate sex education.

One last word is needed. While you want to help children develop necessary inhibitions, you do not want to induce excessive guilt or fear that will prevent them from coming to you for help. First of all, children often do find sexual play pleasant; second, children not only forget rules, but find it confusing to define appropriate behavior. Finally, they may find it hard to tell you about what Uncle Charlie did to them if they're afraid you'll be mad at them, or will hurt Uncle Charlie, whom they like. They need to know ahead of time that you understand how confusing it can be, that you will not be angry if they have forgotten your rules, and that your interest is in protecting them, not hurting someone else. Hence, they can feel free to talk things over with you, even when they're not sure whether anything bad really occurred.

What if my child really has been molested?

Probably nothing stirs up such immediate emotional upheaval as the knowledge that one's child has been molested. But your first task—and possibly your hardest one—in such an event is to remain calm! You know from experience that when a child has been hurt, sweeping him or her up into your arms, screaming and rushing around in panic increases the child's panic. Furthermore, it prevents you from assessing the degree of hurt and taking the necessary steps to provide aid. No matter how badly your heart is thumping you provide calm assurance that whatever happened is over, things are now all right, you are in command, and provide the appropriate amount of comforting.

The same thing is true with molestation. Bearing in mind Schultz's point that emotional damage is far more apt to accrue from adult over-reaction than from the original offense, you will want to quickly provide assurance that the child is now safe, that you are in control, to gauge how upset or hurt the child is, provide immediate comfort, find out both the facts and how the child feels about them. Anything you can do to help the child express feelings such as fear, anger or confusion will be helpful, as will your own empathy, and your assistance in putting the event into perspective.

Here are some examples of comments parents have found to be helpful, either in getting the story or in reacting to it.

"I guess you're pretty scared. But it's okay now—I'm here! Just take your time and when you're feeling a bit calmer, you can tell me exactly what happened."

"I know how mad and scared you are—it makes me mad, too, to think of a grown man trying to frighten someone like that. Good thing most men aren't like that! But you did just right in telling me right away; you try to remember what he looked like, so I can describe him to the police, and then let's have some hot chocolate."

"I know you feel badly telling me about Uncle Charlie. And I feel badly too. But you did the right thing and much as I love him, it's not fair for him to do such things with children. Now that I know about it, I can figure out how to help you. But I won't get you in trouble with Uncle Charlie —I'm sure he feels badly too."

"The baby sitter tried to kiss you? Well, tell me a little more about it. How did it happen? Was it on your forehead like I kiss you? Or did he use his tongue? And was it a game you were playing together that was fun? Or were you just afraid to say no?"

"Now that we know you're okay and not hurt, maybe you're kind of confused about what the man was trying to do and why. I could understand your not even knowing how to feel about it. Sometimes it helps to talk it over a bit more."

"You know, most people aren't that way. Such a thing will probably never happen to you again. But in case it does, here are some things you can do to get help faster."

"I guess you'd like to kill that guy. That was my first reaction too. But you know, people who try to have sex with children are really sad! They do that because they're scared of having sex with adults. And that's too bad, because sex with two loving grownups is a very beautiful thing."

"You know what Aunt Mary did when she was your age and a man tried to show her his penis? She said, 'Yeah, I've seen that before. My father has one too.' And someone else I know said, 'Didn't your mother tell you that penises are private?' It's just like when your brother tries to scare you. If you don't get scared, it takes all the fun away."

"You know, I was just thinking. . .isn't it strange for a grown man to think penises are scarey? That man had no right to try to scare you. But maybe his mother never told him about penises."

All of these comments recognized the child's possible feeling, offered sympathy and protection, yet helped the child put the event into proper perspective and get back to everyday living. What you say will depend on what you think is needed at the moment. And, naturally, common sense enters in—if immediate medical attention is needed, that will be your first priority. Or if the offender is still in the vicinity and the offense was dangerous, calling the police may be first on your agenda.

Tip:

If the police are needed, prepare the child for the realities of police questioning. Explain that the police know that frightened people often get mixed up, but they need to be sure they get the facts straight. Hence, they test people's memories by asking the same questions over and over again, sometimes trying to change what has been said. The child need not get scared, but should just try to remember as well as possible. Police questioning can be the most traumatic part of the whole business, so even though you will want to avoid unnecessary interference, don't hesitate to intervene if you feel that the child is becoming overly upset. A child may have been threatened and fear retribution by the offender, or may have conflicting loyalties. Provide reassurance that you will neither let the offender hurt him or her, nor are you going to hurt the offender, no matter how angry you might be. Your interest is protection, not revenge.

What if my child has been raped?

Rape is an act of violence with such emotional impact that some general discussion is in order before going on. There are other acts of violence that also have emotional impact which may have far more serious physical consequences. Yet we tend to put rape in a special category. We have a greater fear of rape than other types of assault and have a stonger emotional reaction to it. Women restrict themselves and their daughters because of this fear. They feel embarrassed, humiliated, and guilty if they have been raped, but angry and outraged if they have been simply assaulted or robbed.

Family, friends and even the police view the rape victim in a different light; their manner changes to suspicion and disbelief when rape is charged. There are many reasons for such severe reactions, for rape is a complex subject with many psychological, religious and political ramifications. Many writers have pointed out that historically, society has considered it a man's right to impose his will on a woman, and condoned rape as part of the spoils of war symbolizing power, more than lust. Hence, basically many people are reacting to our ideas concerning the sexual rights of a husband over his wife, or the woman's duty to preserve these rights for a future husband. They believe very deeply that the woman has been contaminated. Coupled with the old belief that women are temptresses, such attitudes lead to anger, humiliation and feelings of guilt not only in the victim, but also in the husband and the family charged with the duty to preserve the woman's sexuality for a husband alone. Intellectually we may no longer believe these ideas but emotionally they continue to haunt us. Even some married women are still embarrassed about their bodies and are fearful of expressing their sexuality. Small wonder then that rape becomes so acutely embarrassing both to the victim and to the family.

Our society is gradually becoming more comfortable about sex and women are freeing themselves from narrow definitions of modesty, purity, and morality. If this trend continues and we can remove or at least separate those earlier attitudes about sex from our thinking about rape, might women themselves and their families be more emotionally able to deal with the experience? Might this in turn dilute the potency of rape as a weapon?

These questions in no way suggest that rape should be treated lightly. Yet I cannot help but feel that the suffering of rape victims and their families would be greatly reduced if we as a society focus more on the invasion of physical privacy and violence rather than giving them added emotional turmoil created by our rigid attitudes toward sex.

How does the rape victim react?

People tend to assume that rape victims are always hysterical, and if they aren't, they are probably not particularly upset. But Burgess and Holstrom, Schultz, and rape counsellors feel strongly that almost all rape victims are upset, and may show it in different ways, at various stages. The most common initial reaction is extreme anger, fear, and anxiety—sometimes handled by very visible reactions such as crying, or shaking. Other victims may handle it by denial; i.e., he or she is in a state of shock, can hardly believe what has happened, tries to shut it out, and appears merely irritable, or even quite calm. Often the initial way of reacting is followed by a second reaction. A victim sometimes goes through a stage of depression, general anxiety, suffers from feelings of shame, embarrassment, inability to make decisions, extreme fear of people, or of being alone. Often physical symptoms such as nightmares, stomach upsets, headaches occur. Indeed, many victims are afraid to report the experience, and the rape only comes to light because of such physical complaints. Sometimes guilt becomes a problem as the victim relives the experience, and wonders if there was any way she or he could have handled things differently. Society's attitudes toward rape reinforce this guilt. But as rape counsellors recently pointed out in a conference on rape, people in such a crisis situation are not able to sit down and explore possibilities—they are concerned with survival, react instinctively out of fear, and often the only way of holding themselves together during the attack is to focus on some triviality that is seemingly irrelevant when viewed in retrospect. Hopefully the victim eventually puts the event into perspective and returns to normal. But rape counsellors point out that this may take a long time, and that sometimes a person may undergo a reoccurrence of anxiety and fear long after the experience has been seemingly forgotten.

How can you be helpful to a rape victim?

As mentioned earlier, the greatest help is similar to that provided following a milder form of molestation, an illness, accident, or any other frightening experience. Your first tasks will be to provide assurance that you will now offer protection, to provide comfort, to get the facts as well as possible, using the same warmth, empathy and techniques that we discussed in Chapter 5. If you are the first person to learn of the attack, you will certainly want to get any medical or legal help necessary; counselling and advice from a rape center or social agency will not only be most helpful to the victim, but to you as the parent, and should be obtained if at all possible.

Obviously, here again your spontaneous reaction will depend greatly on your basic attitudes about rape. Again there are myths to be cleared away and information needed before it becomes practical to talk more about what to do or say.

A common myth is that rape victims—particularly women—really want to be raped, and hence either unconsciously or deliberately provoke it or do less than they should to prevent it. The fact that women often have rape fantasies has been cited as proof of their "real" wishes. Another myth is that women will often lie about it in order to protect their reputations or to get even with someone who has angered them.

These possibilities do exist. But they are far less common than is generally supposed. Burgess and Holstrom, in their book *Rape* (1974), discuss a study made of all rape victims seen at Boston City Hospital in one year. They conclude that aside from legal definitions of rape, there are many types of rape, falling within two broad categories: One, a "blitz" rape in which the victim is violently attacked out of the blue by an unknown assailant, and the other a "confidence" rape, in which the rapist gains the victim's trust and then betrays it. Examples of the latter might be that the victim consents to some form of sexual experience but the rapist violates the terms of the agreement; that a child or someone without the mental capacity to judge the situation is bribed, threatened, or convinced that intercourse should not be resisted, or even that the victim agrees in the beginning, changes her or his mind, and is then forced.

No matter what the circumstances leading up to the rape, the rape itself constitutes a violent assault against the will of the victim, which the victim feels powerless to prevent, and which consequently is extremely traumatic. In fact, Schultz reports that the stronger the relationship existing between the victim and the rapist prior to the rape, the more traumatic the attack is apt to be for the victim.

As for the argument about rape fantasies—well, we have less than complete data about sexual fantasies in general, and about women's fantasies in particular. But there is evidence that both men and women have rape fantasies, that generally violence is not really part of such fantasies, and that even people who truly fantasize being physically hurt generally have no wish to have such fantasies translated into reality. There are many theories about the reasons for rape fantasies in women, but since none have been adequately proved, let me share with you the one that makes the most sense to me. For women in general, the right to enjoy sexuality has been a recent development in our society; hence they may only feel comfortable about it in a fantasy situation that enables them to enjoy it without taking responsibility for their actions. This is even more true for the young teenager, for whom it is a beginning step in coming to grips with sexuality. A young girl, for instance, might be interested and curious about intercourse, yet frightened of the actual possibility. A rape in fantasy allows her to say, in essence, "Well, I wouldn't do anything on my own to have intercourse, but if it just happened to me and I couldn't prevent it, that might be all right." In a sense, then, such a fantasy gives one "permission" to have sexual desires. But the girl is not really envisioning being hurt. The fantasy suggests that she might really wish intercourse—it does not necessarily suggest that she might really wish to be violently raped.

Rape counsellors offer this advice: encourage but don't force the victim to talk about his or her feelings. Allow for a period of regression (just as you allow a period of rest and recuperation for an illness) but try not to over-protect; let the person take part in any decisions to be made, encouraging him or her to resume normal activities with as much independence as his or her age allows. Anything else you can say or do to help the person regain a sense of capability and self-esteem will probably speed an ability for him or her to come to terms with the experience. Don't let your own guilt feelings get in the way—many parents think, "Why didn't I give more advice? Why didn't I keep her from going out? Why didn't I. . . .?" But rape is not your fault, any more than it is your child's. You could not predict the future any more than he or she could, nor will you be able to following a rape. Traumatic as it is, rape is still uncommon enough that people need not rule their lives by it, and your confidence in your child's ability to cope with everyday life will be an essential ingredient in his or her future well-being.

Here are some excerpts from reported conversations between rape victims and understanding parents:

Child: Everyone will wonder why I didn't fight harder? All I remember is thinking "I wish I were at home." Isn't that stupid?

Mother: Not at all! You must have been scared half to death, and many people react that way. Besides, you had no way of knowing whether fighting would help you or hurt you.

Child: That's right! I thought he was going to kill me. In fact, now that I think about it, he told me he wouldn't hurt me if I kept quiet. I didn't know what else to do.

Mother: Of course you didn't! You did what you sensed was your best choice, and you were probably right. I would probably have done the same thing. You handled it as well as you could!

• Child: I don't want to ever go to school again. Everybody will know. How will I explain my black eye? I'm so embarrassed.

Father: It will probably be hard the first day but after that it should be easier. You have nothing to be embarrassed about. You have a right to talk or not to talk about your personal experiences, but sometimes it helps to confide in a friend. You may be worrying that people can guess what happened. Remember you look like anyone else who has been hurt and no one can read your thoughts.

Mother: You can use the old joke for those you don't wish to explain to—"A canary bit me." Or you might say that you were attacked and you're not up to talking about it just yet.

● Child: I'm afraid to go to the store alone. What if it happens again?

Father: I know that's a scarey thought! But nothing's apt to happen. If you'd feel better though, until you get your self-confidence back, I'll follow along in the car, just out of sight, but close enough to get to you fast if you need me. We'll take things bit by bit, and soon you won't be as scared.

● Child: I don't ever want to go out with a boy again, much less let one kiss me, if that's what it leads to!

Mother: I can see why you'd feel that way. It may take time and you take as much as you need. But remember, most boys don't act that way, and as you get more experience, you'll be better able to judge the situation. And I'll help you.

All of these comments recognized the child's feelings, accepted them, and yet laid the groundwork for a better perspective. Also, giving specific ways to handle a situation gave the child something concrete to use as needed.

Generally, these principles apply whether the victim is a child, adolescent, or young adult, male or female. But there are variations according to the age, sex, and situation. Very young children, for instance, may be highly confused as to what has happened. They may need an explanation in order to know that adults do not generally assault aimlessly, without warning and for no reason. Teenagers will need much more help in sorting out feelings about sex, and may be more acutely embarrassed and worried about peer reactions. There will be immediate decisions to be made not only about a venereal disease examination and possible prosecution, but about protection against pregnancy for a girl. Often the medical pelvic exams, the police questioning, and entire court procedure—perhaps with unsympathetic lawyers or prose-cutors—is experienced as a second rape, rather than a helpful procedure. So you will need to be supportive and understanding in seeing your child through the whole procedure.

If the attack was a homosexual one, as is usually the case with a boy, the child may need help with some added fears. Teen-agers in particular may worry that they were attacked because they were seen as homosexual, that they will henceforth be viewed by others as homosexual, or that they may indeed *be* homosexual. Boys may feel that their inability to defend themselves was in itself a blow to masculine pride, and that "a real man" would have been able to do so. No matter what the particular worry, the crucial attitude adults need to impart is that rape does not reflect on the masculinity or femininity of the victim.

Handling the aftermath of rape is never easy. While there are no clear-cut preventative measures, you can sometimes help by letting girls know that the provocative game playing that goes on in dates can be misinterpreted as a go-ahead signal, leading to humiliation and anger when a refusal finally occurs, and resulting in rape. You can let boys know that force is never tolerable no matter what the provocation has been!

This might seem like a subject more concerned with adolescence than childhood. But you will need to think about such things ahead of time. Not only are there child rape victims, but your attitudes will show up in everyday conversation, and many a child or teenager has been afraid to even tell what has happened to them because they sensed that their parents would be angry with them.

I hope that the amount of space devoted to this topic will not frighten you needlessly. Child molestation and rape, despite our concern and evidence of its increase, is still a relatively uncommon problem. But because it is such a difficult one for people to deal with, and is so often left out of books like this one, I feel it is worth spending some time on the subject.

CHAPTER SEVEN

USE OF TV, BOOKS, AND MOVIES

Books:

Books, if used well, can be very helpful as either door openers or clinchers. They can also be door closers. The earlier you use them the better, and slipped in along with all other books and read with or to the child, they will be door openers. Then children can reread by themselves when old enough, to refresh their memory or better yet, just for fun.

With older children, from about ten through the teen years, they are better used as clinchers. When you feel you have explained something as well as you can and need a more professional discussion, when you have tried to open doors at some point and failed, or when you want an "expert" to back you up, a book can reinforce and perhaps clarify what you have said. A book can also stimulate discussion. If you just hand books to children and leave them alone, however, they may assume you are deliberately closing the door. But even if they don't assume that, they may make those books their educators, and leave you out entirely. Since no book in the world will agree with you completely, you should know what is in any book you give them and how your children are interpreting it. You may need to use some door openers just to get them to talk about it; for example, you may have to pick out a controversial passage and ask them what they thought of it. If they still don't want to discuss it, it will be hard to open the door they have closed. That is why I provide my child with books to read alone only after I have gone as far as I can at any given point.

Tip:

Try to avoid the cute little books for small children that talk about puppies and kittens, or birds and bees. They seldom get around to talking about people, and children often miss the connection. Or they get there so late that by the time they do, the message has been given that the subject calls for some uneasiness and pussyfooting. Books that talk only about babies are almost as bad. Of course that may be all you want at some point, but I'd look for books with pictures of real people illustrating all the body parts, and discussion of intercourse, as soon as possible. It won't hurt your child and will ease the way for you. For children old enough to read, leaving books around on a shelf accessible to them will enable them to read when they are ready and interested.

Another tip:

Many people assume that they need only one book on sex, whether the book is for children or adults. But no book covers everything, and no two books are given the same perspective or are equally good in every respect. So whether you are using books for children, for adults about children, or for adults about adults, you might want at least two.

And still another tip:

Many people feel that you should not write in books. But there are times when I think that rule can be broken. Using books on sex is one of those times. I consider them equivalents of textbooks, and would buy one I like rather than borrowing it, partly to have it always handy and partly so that I can feel free to write in it.

No matter how much you may like a book, there may be something in it with which you disagree, and unfortunate as it may be, some books can contain absolutely wrong information. Since a child old enough to read alone will not check with you on everything, I consider it quite appropriate to write a comment or a correction in the margin. Here are some examples:

Where Did I Come From? a picture book for beginning readers terms the ejaculate as "sperm" and then describes it as being made of smaller drops of sperm. The ejaculate does contain sperm, but its name is "semen." It has drawings of adults, including the penis, but it does not show or mention the testicles. It further gives an explanation for twins that is only partially true, and is misleading. I would have no hesitancy in writing in the correct label, drawing in some testicles, and noting that the twin explanation is wrong and the child should see you. You can look up the correct explanation together if you wish.

David Reuben's *Everything You Always Wanted to Know About Sex But Were Afraid to Ask* has performed a service to society, I suppose, if only through its clever title that gives people permission to admit they have such questions and to openly seek answers. Further, his list of questions show people that their concerns are similar to others'. I imagine that teenagers will eagerly read that book for many years to come. You should know, however, that the answers, both in this and Dr. Reuben's other writings, have been strongly criticized by many authorities on sexuality. In his own book, *The Sensual Person,* Dr. Albert Ellis has questioned Reuben's material on heterosexual behavior. Many knowledgeable people feel that Reuben presents distortions and half-truths about homosexuality. Some gynecologists I've talked to take strong exception to at least one statement—that Coca Cola is a cheap and effective douche. Still other people, myself included, consider the entire tone of the book somewhat "smirky," admittedly a very subjective evaluation. At any rate, if I found my children reading this book, I'd definitely suggest that they supplement it with readings from other authorities, and I would comment on any statement I thought might be open to question.

If I were a Catholic, I'd certainly appreciate books written from a Catholic point of view. If I were a Catholic who did not agree with the doctrine that masturbation is sinful, I'd feel free to write in, "I (or our priest) disagree," in any book where the author so labeled it. This does not mean you should disagree with Church doctrine, merely that you may want to share your own thinking in areas that have been debated within the Church.

It is best to use such tactics sparingly, or they'll lose effectiveness. Assume that if your comments are more permissive than the author's, they'll serve as door openers that may enable the child to come to you for further discussion. If they are less permissive, they will be apt to act as door closers and be tossed off by the daughter or son as just a parent's hang-up. It would seem wiser to make less permissive comments verbally.

Pictures:

Many people worry about how explicit pictures should be. One sales clerk even tried to talk me out of buying *Where Did I Come From?* because the illustrations, hardly sexy ones, showed a father with a penis. Children learn visually. The more they see what bodies look like in books and pictures, the less need they'll have to seek information through exploration with other people. The older they become, the more they will need illustrations as realistic as possible.

The Sex Book is a pictorial encyclopedia that may be useful for the whole family. It may be too explicit for some tastes, and even the authors now wish they had done some things differently. The photographs are all of Caucasians, some are so arty that they may be unintelligible, and some are misplaced and captionless, hence may seem irrelevant to the text. But it provides concise definitions, thoughtful text, and informative photographs on an extremely wide variety of subjects. If left on a shelf or table accessible to children, they can thumb through it when they wish. One youngster had trouble with his father's explanation of ejaculation. He understood it only when he saw a photograph that showed it; and while that photograph in no way stimulated him sexually, it did clear up his confusion.

Movies:

Audio-visual aids enhance learning in most subjects. After all, don't we all enjoy learning our history far more in television dramas and movies than we do through dry textbooks and treatises on the Constitution? Sex is no exception. In fact, movies may be even more useful in this area, for they help us to comprehend processes and behaviors difficult to conceptualize, and provide information to help us function more efficiently. With most behavior, for instance, we learn by comparing our own behavior to that of others.

In sexual matters, we don't have much opportunity for such observation. We are not apt to show or discuss with others how we perform intercourse, for instance, nor are others apt to show or discuss such intimacies with us. Hence pictures and movies, particularly educational ones, but also those meant for entertainment or even those honestly pornographic, may be the only way we can learn about sexual behaviors through observation.

Educational Films:

There are many good films designed for use in the class-room, and it is helpful for little children, in-betweeners, and adolescents to see not only diagrams on reproduction, but movies of real people, with and without clothes, dealing with various aspects of sexuality appropriate for their particular ages. By the time they are seniors or even juniors in high school, I see nothing wrong in their viewing educational films showing inter-course, recognizing that they may be embarrassed at first, or even briefly sexually aroused.

In the first place, by that time, whether we like it or not, many of those students will already be having intercourse. In the second place, truly educational films discuss topics that need discussion, give correct information, stress sexuality in a loving, beautiful relationship, and are a much better introduction to explicitness than pornography or commercial X-rated films. Further, they are often designed to promote discussion, and for adolescents and adults alike, act as "desensitizers" and "looseners" to enable people to talk more easily about sex.

While films on heterosexuality are probably more useful to the majority of students, I also see no harm in showing films on homosexuality to high school juniors or seniors. Some of those students will have already engaged in homosexual behavior, may have already considered themselves homosexual, or may be in considerable conflict about it. Both they and their classmates can benefit from seeing and hearing honest portrayals of homo-sexuality and bisexuality.

Of course any film can be misused. Taken out of context or seen without adequate discussion, it can be upsetting and less than helpful. Hence many such films are made available only to professionals for class or workshop purposes. Even educators in adult classes will seldom allow people to enter the class merely to see a film. Parents might well question the legitimacy of any "class" that shows explicit films without proper leadership and discussion. Note here that I am talking about "explicitness," not "pornography"—the two words are not synonymous.

Food for Thought:

Some sex educators are beginning to suggest that explicit films be made available on tapes, to be rented out to families and viewed in the privacy of their own homes. I think this might be very useful, at least if done in conjunction with an ongoing class. What do you think?

Popular Movies:

It must be obvious by now that I don't worry too much about taking children to see movies that have a bit about sex in them. For one thing, this makes "sex" just a part of everything else, and hence it becomes less special, exciting, and over-emphasized than we have made it in the past. For another, it is so useful as a door opener—it both provides information and leads to discussion that might ordinarily be difficult for either a child or parent to initiate. Further, it teaches through modeling. Children learn attitudes by whether their parents laugh, are disgusted, or show no reaction at all. If a scene might be frightening, it is reassuring for children to have their parents there to explain and remain calm.

Does this mean that children should see all movies? Of course not! One would hope that parents would use a bit of common sense and until the middle teens, avoid movies that are extremely explicit, violent, or so beyond comprehension that they might be badly misinterpreted. But for the most part, it will be mostly the "middle" ages and early teens, i.e., from around ages nine or ten to thirteen or possibly fourteen, that might be adversely affected. Smaller children will usually not understand it, and unless it is violent, will be mainly bored. The middle teenagers from fourteen on up will be sneaking into objectionable films anyhow. I'd rather have them see such films with responsible adults who can offset the problems, than with snickering, equally confused friends. For that matter, I would rather have my children see some adult movies for developing a healthy attitude toward sex, than some of the so-called family movies that deal with sex by snickering and coy inuendos, that make it cute for tiny tots to act like dating teenagers and present unrealistic and romanticized attitudes about sex and love.

One problem many parents have is trying to explain to children why they are not being allowed to see an R or X rated film. I actually think that's easier to explain if you have allowed them to see some shows, and they know you've got some basis for your thinking other than that they are "too young." They'll be more apt to trust your judgment, even if they don't understand or agree with it. Sometimes, it is even helpful to let them learn through a mistake.

My son, at around eleven, accepted an explanation that a particular movie was too mature for him, when reminded that he had been pretty bored in the last one he had seen. A few months later he grudgingly accepted the rationale that I felt he was getting the idea that all sex was violent, and I'd prefer he not go with us to a certain film. Finally, with a movie that was unknown to us, he begged to be allowed to take his chances. We agreed, and sure enough, it turned out to have a somewhat explicit, unnecessary and objectional rape scene. Later he confided that he had been embarrassed and scared, and next time he would listen to me. At least our discussion about the scene was helpful to him. His friends who sneaked into that movie had no such advantage. A couple of years later, the publicity on a certain X film made every teenager around beg to see it. I objected, but my kids pointed out they were now "older," had our attitudes ingrained in them, and if they got scared, it would be their own fault. They turned out to be right. The movie neither frightened them as it was meant to do, nor did it affect their attitudes toward sex. They considered it vulgar, disgusting and a "rip off." They made no further requests to see X films until they were almost old enough to fit the standard age requirements, had enough judgment to decide for themselves what they wish to see, and as far as I could tell, showed better judgment than that of the official "raters."

This does not mean there are no risks. One can never predict what might embarrass or upset a particular child at a particular age. We found out eventually, for instance, that movies that had concerned us had not bothered our children at all, while movies we thought were beautiful had embarrassed them a lot. Still, they were going to get embarrassed at their first display of nudity in a film no matter what, so we were glad that it occurred in a movie we felt good about, and where we could model positive feelings about "positive" sexuality.

Other than that, the risks are mainly for the parent, and if one takes a child to a movie with sex in it, he or she had better have a good sense of humor. Not only is it a hassle to stop and explain in the middle of a fast moving film, but one never can tell what will happen next.

Our son's first encounter with a PG film was with an early Woody Allen movie. There was nothing more sexy than a funny scene of Woody Allen ineptly fumbling with buttons while trying to make love. My son, who had never been known for quiet whispers, said, "Mom, what is he doing?" I mumbled a hurried answer; there was a short silence, and then, "Did Dad do that to you?" There were some chuckles in the row behind us, and I rather sank down in my seat as I said, "Yes," praying that Woody Allen would say something uproariously funny. He didn't; instead my son's loud "YUCK!" resounded through the theater, and Woody Allen's next joke, when it finally came, was completely upstaged.

His next one was a warm delightful movie about a man who took a twelve year old with him on a weekend of wine, women and song. Their final destination was to be a "cathouse." My son waited expectantly, asking frequently, "Is it the 'cathouse' yet? When is it going to be a 'cathouse'?" When the hero and his young charge finally wandered through a room filled with women in various stages of undress, my son kept saying, "Is that the 'cathouse'? You're sure that's the 'cathouse'?" Once the scene was over, there was a short silence, and into that silence roared a disappointed "GEE WHIZ! All it was was a bunch of women! I thought it was going to be CATS!" The audience burst into laughter; next time we went to an R movie, we got a baby sitter.

Television:

Parents are becoming increasingly concerned about the effects of television. While it is certainly better to have some things after bedtime hours, I think the same general principles apply here as did to movies. Children will be bored, if too young, by most material on sex, and if old enough to be interested, are probably ready to see it and can benefit from parental discussion. I would prefer a good explicit educational film on natural childbirth, even for a young child, to the mysterious, inaccurate and often frightening allusions to childbirth that occur in many family programs. I welcome the recent trend in many cities to allow advertising of condoms. I would suggest merely that parents anticipate the kinds of questions that their children might ask when they see the ads, and that they have their sense of humor as well as their answers ready.

Seeing a well done program that includes casual but honest talk about sex, or that really tackles such subjects as homosexuality, new lifestyles and rape can be quite useful for older children and teenagers. Television has some distinct advantages over movies; for one thing, it allows children to ask questions or discuss things with parents either during the program or the commercial, without ruining parental enjoyment or annoying an audience. For another, it allows them to walk around or do other things while half watching, and parents can call them in to watch a particular program segment and then let them leave. Since they can come and go at will, even adult education programs can become useful. If a family has two television sets, children who are embarrassed have the option of watching by themselves, in private, and asking questions later.

What does concern me are sexist attitudes imparted via commercials and many programs. Misleading advertising also preys on adolescent worries. An example is a commercial which suggests the "right" toothpaste or vaginal deodorants are necessary to be sexually acceptable. I would certainly protest if advertising for condoms becomes misleading. Although I'm glad to see advertisements for menstrual supplies make the subject more discussable, I'd far prefer the correct terms than the phony euphemisms created in the name of "good taste." There are many other things I dislike too; but I'd rather have my children see them on TV at home when I have the ability to interject my own opinions, than to have all such unplanned sex education come from other sources, without my knowledge.

Pornography:

Few topics evoke as much controversy as pornography. Parents worry that it will frighten or overstimulate children, or even worse, provoke criminal behavior in teenagers and adults. Yet 85 percent of the men and 70 percent of the women in the United States see explicit erotic material, most of them by the time they reach the ages of fifteen to eighteen. Most of them grow into responsible, well adjusted people. So let's try to answer some of the questions people have about it.

Just what is pornography?

In using the term, we probably all envision the vulgar explicitness of hard core books, pictures and movies. Finding a legal definition that differentiates between explicitness, art, literature, education and pornography, however, without destroying civil liberties, poses one of the most puzzling dilemmas our courts face.

Attempts to use intent to sexually arouse the reader or viewer, to use actual arousal, to use quality and taste, or to use socially redeeming value as criteria have proved fruitless. It is often impossible to know what an author or artist had in mind. What arouses one person may not another. Quality and taste differ from generation to generation, person to person, and place to place. Recent attempts to let each community make its own decision have led to fine educational material being banned in some cities, and hard core pornography allowed in others. The difficulty the Supreme Court has had suggests that a definition satisfactory to all may be impossible to achieve.

Who enjoys it?

Do only old men or emotionally disturbed people enjoy pornography? Well, it's true that such people sometimes enjoy it. So do women, young, middle-aged and older adults of both genders, adolescents, wealthy, educated, and "well adjusted" people. Interest in pornography is found in all segments of the population.

What are its advantages?

It can help adults who have difficulty becoming sexually aroused improve their sexual functioning. There is evidence that it may help some people handle unacceptable sexual impulses through fantasy and masturbation, thus reducing their potential for harming others. It is a most effective way to show people that any thought they may have had has also occurred to others, thus relieving inappropriate guilt feelings.

What are its disadvantages?

First, much of today's pornography provides misinformation. Sexual positions may be grotesquely exaggerated, and models are often chosen for their superior physical endowments. Young teenagers looking for information can receive distorted ideas of how people look and how they should behave in a sexual relationship. That's another reason for producing and showing explicit sex education movies and pictures that are truly informative. The more adequate information teenagers have, the less their need to turn to pornography.

Second, most pornography today communicates poor values by insidiously teaching and reinforcing ideas that pervade our society. It gives sex little meaning other than a physical act out of the context of a human relationship. It often associates sex with exploitation and violence. It especially exploits women by being designed almost exclusively to excite men and reinforcing the idea that women enjoy being seduced or even raped. Even if women were allowed to be the exploiters, the idea that people should be "used" hardly encourages trust and caring. Indeed, warmth, affection, and caring are generally absent in pornography.

What effect does pornography have on adults and children?

After a thorough study, the President's Commission on Obscenity and Pornography in 1970 concluded that pornography was neither harmful to adults nor caused criminality in either adults or youth. While there was less information about the effects on children, they found no evidence that exposure to pornography had a detrimental effect on moral character, sexual orientation, or attitudes. There seems little need, then, for the exaggerated fear held by many people.

On the other hand, we may well be concerned that our research has been inadequate, and that there are indeed harmful effects—especially for children or early adolescents—that are just not easily researched. Many adults relate the confusion or fright that pornography caused them as young teenagers. More important, to the extent that pornography gives unplanned sex education which teaches disregard for human worth and dignity, it may indirectly condone physical and emotional violence.

What should we do about pornography?

I think we need an attitude of active but rational concern. We should be aware that children may see pornography no matter how we try to protect them, and try to provide education that dilutes its destructive potential. For example, rather than rushing children past theaters, confiscating material you find or panicking if your children find any that you have, you'll be more helpful if you use these occasions as door openers to the sex education you really wish to provide.

Concerned as I am about pornography's messages, I do not agree that trying to define it in order to completely ban it, thereby adding to its exciting mystique, is a useful or viable solution. After all, we receive sexism and violence through our literature and movies continually. We don't try to eliminate movies and books, we try to change their content.

It seems more useful to me to settle for a definition of pornography as any material that either intentionally or unintentionally arouses someone, and concentrate on trying to change both the nature of destructive pornography and the advertisements given it. We can all add to societal planned sex education by seeking legislation to protect children from being used as pornographic subjects and prevent merchants from allowing and encouraging children to see material meant only for adults. We can crowd out destructive pornography by demanding and giving youth access to explicit material which, whether recreational or educational, is honest, non-exploitative, and which treats sex as a warm and loving part of life. Until society reaches that goal, you yourself, through calm preventive and corrective comments, can provide planned sex education that helps youth distinguish between art and trash.

It may help to know that according to research, repeated or prolonged exposure to explicit material tends to decrease sexual stimulation, and often leads to boredom. My husband and I were in Denmark just after pornography became legal there. It was discreetly displayed in store windows. We noted with some interest that couples would stroll by with their children, pausing briefly to look in those windows. While they looked, their children stood on the sidewalk shifting impatiently, just as ours did when we looked in camera stores. If there was a candy store around, the children rushed over to look at the candy while their parents looked at the pornography. Nobody seemed much bothered. We learned later that the pornography business had already begun to dwindle. The major lookers and buyers were curious West Germans and Americans, not the already bored Danes.

CHAPTER EIGHT

REACHING YOUR ADOLESCENT

If you are the parent of a teenager, you have probably already discovered that you are the most useless, rejected, stupid, embarrassing, square, and all-round incompetent person in the world, except, of course, momentarily, when you have just handed over the keys to the family car or an advance on next week's allowance. Just remember that if you always seem that way to your offspring it may be because deep down that's the way they feel about themselves. Teenagers more often than anyone else in the world consider themselves "different," isolated and lonely, even when they are the carbon copy of their friends and are surrounded by them.

They worry about everything. They are anxious about whether they are too thin or too fat, too tall or too short, have penises or breasts that are too little or too big, menstruate too early or too late, or are too ugly or too—yes, it is possible—pretty. No matter how right you may be, their friends know more than you do. They don't want to even be seen with you, much less caught showing affection to you, for fear they will be considered "babies," or so unpopular that they are reduced to going out with parents.

They want to be told "no" and they want to be told "yes," but no matter which you do, they will say they wanted the opposite. Sometimes you will have to let them "blame it on you," so that they can save face if caught in a situation they really can't handle. The sexual revolution will not prevent them from going through the same confusions that all teenagers have gone through, but it may make them face those confusions earlier than you did, when they are even less able to handle them. They will need your patience and understanding, even though at times they won't deserve them. They will also need your strength, even though they will make saying "no" unbearably difficult.

One reason for the problems in adolescence is that while the complexities of today's society place teenagers in a child-like role they are faced with adult sexual needs and are expected to develop adult responsibilities. In Biblical times, adolescence was not such a problem. When a child reached "the teens" he or she automatically became a member of the adult community, with both its rights and its obligations. That may have been frightening at times, but it was certainly less confusing.

Another problem in adolescence is the almost universal difficulty that parents and children seem to have in seeing each other as sexual beings. There is probably no taboo as universal as that of incest. Yet many parents, to their horror, find themselves with sexual feelings toward their teenage son or daughter that they never meant to have. Moreover, the adolescent may feel the same way toward them. Some of the friction between parent and adolescent comes because both parties are so ashamed of these feelings that they will go to any length to deny them and hence shut out all positive feelings between them. Or conversely, sometimes a child becomes so close to the parent of the opposite sex that the parent of the same sex feels left out. Either way, somebody is left feeling hurt and angry. It may help to know that this is a part of growing up. For the teenager, it is a transition into developing feelings toward the opposite sex, while playing out the inevitable conflicts on the safest people around, Mama and Papa.

And how about you? Why shouldn't you have sexual feelings? Your child is suddenly looking like an adult, and possibly similar to the one you fell in love with twenty years ago. Your unacceptable thoughts are merely proof that you have successfully brought your child to near adulthood, and he or she will have to be thought of and treated as more adult than child from now on. The chances of committing incest are small, and unless translated into behavior, your feelings are not in themselves harmful.

QUESTIONS PEOPLE ASK ABOUT ADOLESCENTS

At what age should children start dating? What deadlines should there be?

At least one study has suggested that the earlier people start dating, and the greater the number of partners, dates, and "steady" relationships they have during high school and college, the more apt they are to engage in premarital intercourse. Yet, there is still no correct starting age for dates, or a "right way" to date. Children differ greatly in their ability to handle dates. While I think fourteen or fifteen sound good, it will depend entirely on you, your child, the type of date in question, and the custom in your community. Moreover, what is meant by the term "date" differs according to age and locale.

In Honolulu recently many parents learned belatedly and to their great surprise, that while their children were not dating at the age of fifteen, they had "gone with" members of the opposite sex at far younger ages. "Going with" had included hand holding, buying sodas at a nearby drugstore, and kissing, all during school hours and completely unknown to parents. Some parents even found that their non-dating children had managed to achieve pregnancies and venereal disease on their non-dates. It is well to keep that in mind if you are tempted to withhold information about such things as birth control on the grounds that your children are not yet dating.

Obviously then, curfews will not prevent teenagers from engaging in "after-hours" behavior. Still, I think some deadlines are important, if for no other reason than to tell children that you are concerned about their welfare. It is also important for them to have limits to serve as guidelines and to fall back on should they find themselves unable to handle a particular situation. What is reasonable for one child may not be for another, and every parent of a teenager learns quite quickly that no matter how permissive he or she is, "Everybody else's parent" is more so. There will be times when they will desperately want you to be firm but will be incapable of letting you know it.

I would suggest that the decision then be based partly on your own thinking and intuition, partly on your estimate of your own child, and partly on discussion with other parents. If you are not yet the parent of a teenager, you may as well know now that it will be a time filled with acting wishy-washy when you are feeling firm and acting firm when you are feeling wishy-washy; it will be a time when that thing everyone else calls common sense will elude you. If you have already discovered that, know that you are not alone, and make the most of that fact. While you will need to guard against invasion of your child's privacy, try comparing notes, mutual handholding, commiseration and discussion of issues with other parents and friends. It is probably the only thing that keeps parents of teenagers rational. The same thing applies to the teenagers about their parents. So gather your friends around for mutual help and support, set your own guidelines for your own children, stick to them, and loosen your rules bit by bit as your children prove that they can abide by them. I suspect that if they have had a fair amount of dating and you have reallly talked with them, they will be able to use their own judgment by the time they are juniors or seniors in high school. However, they should still be expected to respect the rules you set for your household.

How do I handle "Don't you trust me?" routines?

"Don't you trust me?" "What can happen after midnight that wouldn't happen before?" and "Are you worried about me or about what the neighbors will think?" are just some more of those questions that inspire nebulous answers. These questions usually come up in regard to deadlines, allowing girls and boys to be in the house alone, whether to make bedrooms off limits, or turning lights off and leaving young people unchaperoned at parties. While sometimes they are guilt provoking routines, they are also valid questions, with no pat answers. You will need a lot of soul searching, honesty and empathy. But here are some thoughts that may help.

The issue is not necessarily one of trust, but rather of recognition of human psychology. Long dates eventually leave people with little to say or do together, and it becomes difficult to know when or how to end a necking session. Sometimes curfews make it easier to end, especially if one person sees intercourse as the end goal, and the other one doesn't.

No matter how you may trust your daughter, girls who have no curfews are given more hassles. Also, the later the hour, the more both boys and girls are subject to hassles from strangers.

Peer pressure inevitably leads to increased necking during parties when parents leave or when lights are turned out. Not only are you concerned about your own children, but you are held accountable to other parents for what has happened to their children in your house.

Empty houses and bedrooms are more conducive to sexual activity than non-empty ones and living rooms, and trust notwithstanding, many teenagers' first experiences with intercourse take place not in cars, but in their own homes while parents are away.

What one does is one's own business. But what neighbors or friends think is still important, if only because a bad reputation can create a lot of unhappiness for your son or daughter.

In the end, you have absolutely no control over what your teenagers do sexually, no matter how many rules you set, short of locking them up in a closet for several years. They will decide and then must take responsibility for what they wish to do with their own bodies. All you can do is provide information and values to help them make decisions, and then do whatever you can to keep them from being pressured, either physically or emotionally, into doing something they really don't want to do or that they may regret later. Your rules are your way of taking your responsibility, the rest of the responsibility is theirs.

Should I give or insist on contraceptives?

I would not give or insist on anything regarding birth control, other than information and values. After all, you are trying to teach your children to take responsibility for their own bodies. You can only take responsibility for yours. That doesn't mean you can't provide an occasional "gift" of some condoms or a female contraceptive to ease the strain on a young person's pocketbook, once he or she has made the decision.

Will discussing details of contraception, encouraging use of it, or helping pay for it push teenagers into having intercourse?

Many studies have shown that mere knowledge about sexual behavior and contraception has little effect on subsequent sexual behavior. Indeed, Kinsey found that less than half of the unmarried women he interviewed listed fear of pregnancy as a deterrent to premarital intercourse. More recent studies have shown that when such subjects were left uncovered by the parents, there was more pre-marital intercourse by girls. This does not mean that freedom from fear of pregnancy has no influence, or that you will never be encouraging intercourse in your actions. It merely means that if you are clear about your wishes and values, giving facts about birth control and encouraging its use during intercourse will not in and of itself lead directly to intercourse.

Is the giving of facts about birth control enough to prevent a teenager from becoming pregnant or getting venereal disease?

More and more research has begun to prove that facts are definitely *not* enough to prevent either problem. We have labored under the delusion that they are for so long, that it's hard to stress this point enough. Even though withholding information seems to increase the problem, there are many many people who have unwanted pregnancy or unwanted venereal disease despite the fact that they are very well informed and believe wholeheartedly in birth control. Here are some of the reasons:

Many women do not consider it immoral to be "swept away" by "love" or "emotion," but do consider it immoral to have "premeditated" sex. Using or carrying a contraceptive on a date, they reason, is planning ahead to have intercourse, removes "sex" from "love," and is therefore guilt provoking.

Many women fear that if they are caught with a contraceptive in their pocketbook, they will be assumed to be willing for intercourse on a date.

The use of a condom, diaphram, or foam is seen as interfering with both the spontaneity and pleasure of intercourse.

Some men and women fear that to request protection from either pregnancy or venereal disease will be considered an insult.

A few people will risk pregnancy because of underlying emotional problems. It may be a way of proving one's masculinity or femininity, a way of seeking affection, or even a way of expressing anger.

Some people feel that abortion is less immoral than contraception.

These attitudes are present in adults as well as teenagers. They will be especially hard to overcome for teenagers, who are more subject to peer pressure than probably any other age group.

Hence the commitment to using contraception or protection against venereal disease will hardly be strong enough to offset them, unless you have incorporated your values throughout your children's lives. You will need to make it very clear to your son or daughter that you consider having unwanted babies or venereal disease a far worse problem to handle than the possibility of an unintended insult. You must be sure they understand that "pleasure" does not replace the need for responsibility, that planning ahead is no more immoral than having unwanted babies, and that abortion, even if you approve of it, is a *last* resort, not a *first* one. You will need to be very clear about one more point: birth control is a responsibility of both. If one partner does not take it, the other one will have to.

Tip:

If you cannot approve contraception other than the rhythm method because of religious convictions, you will need to be clear about your values and especially informative about its use. Even religious people engage in premarital sex, and the rhythm method is not very effective even when used well. Used poorly, it is mainly effective in creating babies, not preventing them.

One might note here that contraceptives are not merely used for contraception. The Pill can be used to regulate menstrual periods or for other medical purposes, although there are increasing questions about its physical side effects for some women. A condom (rubber) can be used also to prevent VD. It is a prevention against syphillis, and is the only form of contraception to provide such protection.

How much do I really want to know about my child's sex life? Does honesty help or hurt?

Certainly all people have private lives which they do not share with parents or spouses. Faced with conflicting emotions about today's changing sexual patterns, parents often (and understandably) take one extreme or another. Either they insist on knowing every little detail, or they throw up their hands and shut their eyes, saying, "I don't want to know what my kids are doing! I couldn't change anything, I'd just get upset, so let them do what they want! All I ask is that I don't know about it!"

The first way not only invades privacy, but is an *a priori* assumption of guilt that may lead children to say, "Well, if I'm going

to be assumed guilty, I might as well have the fun to go with it."
It certainly does not enhance the kind of good communication
necessary for helpful sex education.

While it's obvious that detailed questioning is a poor way to
handle the problem, it's harder to gauge at what point questioning becomes an invasion of privacy. You must ask yourself—what
do I really need to know? There are no easy answers to that—just
a hint that if your questioning seems to be closing doors instead of
opening them, you might as well decide that it's time to use a bit
more empathy, honesty about the reasons for your questions, try
some door opening at points, and temporarily lay low, put adhesive
tape on your mouth, and try to have a little trust.

The "I don't want to know" approach poses other problems
and questions even more difficult to react to. Certainly the research on the helpfulness of honest sharing is confusing. On the
one hand, studies show that it is helpful to teenagers to be able to
talk honestly and openly with parents. In fact, one study, noting
the difficulty parents and children have in seeing each other as
sexual beings and the misconceptions of each other that give rise
to a "generation gap," found evidence that when mothers and
daughters honestly share their sexual values and experiences, it is
helpful to both. But another study with another set of mothers
and daughters found the opposite to be true—that confronted with
both the sexuality of their daughters and the generation gap in
values, mothers became so upset that it closed off communication
and made things worse.

Such contradictory studies leave parents with the realization
that there is still much we do not know, and that we will have to
struggle through, finding our own happy mediums. My own thinking is that there is a happy medium partly based on one's own
abilities: certainly you should not ask questions if you are not
willing to hear the answers. But if sticking one's head in the sand is
easier on parents, it is not helpful to children, who are then left
uncertain about parental values and expectations, and who have
no guidelines or help with problems. You *do not* need to know
every last detail. You do need to know enough about what your
kids are doing to know their struggles and how to help them. And
they need to know that when you ask, you are doing so not out

of lack of trust, but from concern for them and willingness to help.

How much impact does a parent really have?

Some parents operate under the mistaken notion that they have tremendous influence in sex education. Others wonder if it's worth trying—if they have any influence at all. Some are aware of their limits of influence and use them carefully.

Again, research, which should tell us the answers, can be confusing. One thing is quite apparent: Despite the fact that we think we place a lot of emphasis on sex education in the home, parents have had far less impact than they realize, even in the sexual revolution. Kinsey found in 1948 that children learned most of what they knew from other children. In 1970, Morton Hunt found that little had changed since Kinsey's time. Two-thirds of the males interviewed and four-fifths of the females stated that they had received no information from their fathers before or during high school; three-fourths of the males and over one-half of the females said the same thing of their mothers. Of those who said they had received some information from parents, most felt that it had been too little, too late, and too superficial. Most studies confirm his finding that friends are still the major source of information and values, reading is second (but far less in importance), parents a poor third, and schools run an even poorer fourth. More surprising is the fact that the younger interviewees tend to give the same responses as older ones.

It seems discouraging, doesn't it!

It seems to authorities on sexuality that we have paid lip service to the concept of helpful sex education while doing little or nothing. It must seem to parents, who have been trying their best, that "trying" is fruitless.

But cheer up, parents. Despite these findings, it is also clear from research that many children do receive a good deal of help from parents. The more adequate information and values are given about a wide range of subjects, the more influence parents have.

Moreover, it is possible that the statistics cited do not tell the whole story. While the studies show how children often perceive the kind of help they were given, such perceptions may have little to do with what has actually taken place. Whether information was given poorly, not at all or with poor timing, or whether

the children were just not able to use it we have no way of knowing. If sex education is viewed on the broad spectrum of influences I have suggested earlier, rather than as purely formal instruction, the most useful education may have been so casually
and informally given, that it was incorporated into a child's total
life, and paving the way for evaluating information received
from many sources. Thus the parent may have been giving sex
education without a child realizing it, and it would have not been
reflected in the studies. In the end, parents and teachers probably
have both more and less influence than they think.

There is ample evidence that when school programs in various
communities have dealt adequately with sexual information, the
incidence of unwed pregnancy and venereal disease has decreased.
While we know now that some parents and teachers have not been
as helpful as they might, we also know that it is both necessary for
them to discuss a wider range of subjects, stressing both direct
information and examining values, and that it is worth the effort
to do so.

CULTURAL VARIATIONS, MYTHOLOGIES, AND TEENAGERS

The cultural variations and influences on sexual behaviors
and attitudes are so important that it would take another book to
deal with them adequately. It's worth at least commenting that
each culture has its own variations, and that in the area of sex
even more than in other areas, we tend to be ethnocentric. We are
apt to say and feel "My way is right, yours is wrong." From our
lack of understanding, we develop a lot of mythologies and stereotypes about various racial and ethnic groups' sexual behavior. If
you are going to be around people from another culture, it is well
to realize this. As a parent dealing with your child's friend, you
can misinterpret some type of behavior and hurt someone's
feelings. As a doctor, teacher, social worker, psychologist, community volunteer, you can fail in your job, undermine someone's
self esteem, set in motion disrupting behavior in the person's
family, or otherwise unintentionally harm someone merely because you did not understand his or her cultural background.
You can undermine a planned sex education program with ignorance or prejudice. Conversely, you can be a lot of help to teenagers (who are especially vulnerable because of their need to be
like everybody else) by exposing and explaining sexual stereotypes

and myths about various racial or ethnic groups. Here are some examples:

Male foreign college students are often confused and embarrassed when accused of being homosexual because they are seen walking hand in hand with a male friend. This is a common and accepted expression of friendship, nothing more, in many countries.

Although ghetto areas may have more unwed pregnancies than some other areas, many of the families have very rigid moral standards for their daughters. Thus one cannot assume that young women coming from such a cultural or community background are sexually promiscuous. In one chicano area for instance, girls were often harrassed by boys who assumed they were "easy lays," or humiliated by chance and thoughtless remarks by teachers or friends' parents.

Often community center programs for teenagers have floundered because a leader failed to reassure the parents whose customs demanded chaperoning that there would be adequate adult supervision for a center party.

People are beginning to realize how unjustly many black males are treated because of myths about their sexual prowess and interest in white females. Other ethnic persons may not realize how damaging this is to black males' own self image, or how myths of sexual superiority create problems within the black community itself. Upon hearing that I was writing a book about sex, one very handsome young black man said to me, "Please put in your book the fact that not all blacks are superstuds, nor do we have twelve-inch penises. Trying to live up to those myths has caused me more trouble than anything else." On the other hand, black girls have often told me that dates who are trying to live up to the superstud image cause them a great deal of trouble.

Worry about breast and penis size is common to all teenagers. But trying to live up to another culture's standards of beauty is especially hard on one's ego, and mythologies complicate matters. Many Asian girls tape their eyelids or undergo plastic surgery in order to look Caucasian. They worry that their breasts are not as large as other ethnic groups. White boys (and men) envy blacks' reportedly long penises, Asians become concerned that they measure up to neither whites nor blacks, and blacks fear they will not measure up to their fellow blacks.

No matter what group they come from, worry about such matters is one of the biggest problems for teenagers. You can help by telling them these facts: Any differences between erect penises either individually or racially, are not that significant. It is unfortunate that some men need so much reassurance about this. Research indicates that men's perceptions of their own penises tends toward "reducing": i.e., they see themselves as smaller than they are. Big penises are neither necessary to satisfy women sexually, nor do they ensure that one will be a good lover. Far more important is good communication, concern, and respect for a partner's needs. Also big breasts are not necessary to be sexually attractive; standards of beauty are relative and change often. Rather than trying to live up to another culture's standards, it is better to appreciate and make the most of the beauty in one's own ethnic features.

SEXISM IN PARENTS

Despite our women's liberation movement, we still practice sexism in our sex education, and probably will for some time to come. Parents often consider it their duty to help boys achieve manhood via the bed. No matter how "liberal" they may be, they often feel that they have failed as parents if they have not managed to preserve their daughter's virginity until marriage. They give a lot of their values to daughters, but very little in the way of either information or values to sons. They assume that boys will learn easily on their own, and will then act as "teachers" to girls. But they are very unhappy if others' sons begin to "teach" their own daughters. Many parents allow boys much more freedom regarding hours, money, and the use of cars than they do girls, and in many other ways show their sexist attitudes.

We might do some real thinking here—is it possible that parents have created needless problems because of their double standards? That many of our worries would be eliminated if we just granted girls the same options as boys from the very beginning?

Some parents with whom I have talked and whom I consider very moral and responsible have begun to tell their fifteen year old daughters that they are now old enough to be responsible for their own bodies and behavior. The daughters are given permission to do whatever they wish sexually, but also given the information and values to go with such freedom. These parents are not at all concerned about the idea that their daughters as well as their sons might be having intercourse. Those whose children are now old enough for adequate evaluation, report that their daughters behaved just as responsibly and morally as any other daughters, if not more so.

SEXUAL RIGHTS OF TEENAGERS

Does a teenager have the right to counselling or help regarding abortion or venereal disease? The Supreme Court has said yes; but that may fail to comfort parents who fear that their children may get bad advice, and who themselves want the right to be known as concerned parents and to take part in important decisions. It may help to know that most agencies have ethical counsellors who know that sometimes teenagers misinterpret parental attitudes, and who do their best to bring parents into the picture. Good professional counsellors do not treat these subjects lightly.

Despite my concerns as a parent, I have handled this by giving my children permission to get such help if needed and if they feel they cannot come to me for guidance. Much as I would want to help them, and concerned as I might be that they felt unable to talk with me, I would rather have them get the help they need than suffer through alone, and would not want them to feel guilty about doing it. My reasons, as well as my permission have been shared with them. Some of the saddest calls I get as a counsellor are from teenage boys who, afraid to really come for help, sneak in an anonymous telephone call while their parents are out. They are convinced that their parents will not talk about sex at all, hence can hardly be expected to be understanding about their worries about such things as masturbation or homosexuality. They have a right to informed, intelligent and concerned answers. Sad as it is that they do not get the help they need, it seems even sadder that probably many of their parents would gladly talk with them, and are merely afraid to broach the subject.

A basic issue here, though, is really do teenagers have sexual rights? Do they have charge over their own bodies? Would they act less like "boys" and "girls" if adults treated them more like the "men" and "women" they are physically? Should economic dependence prevent them from enjoying the sexual rights available to others who are only a few years older?

One last thought:

Dealing with adolescents is often not easy for either the parent or the child. But if both parties are willing, talking about sex can provide some of the warmest, closest moments together that a parent and child can have.

CHAPTER NINE

WHAT EVERY YOUNG COUPLE SHOULD KNOW—
THAT PARENTS OFTEN FORGET TO TELL

Eventually most children grow up and get married; and tradition says that the parents should give them a word or two of advice about sex before the wedding. The timing may seem rather outmoded today, when a high proportion of brides and grooms will have already been living together, or will have had a fair a-mount of sexual experience. Whether your adult children are getting married, living together, or merely having sexual relationships, the information that follows will be useful. But since a wedding provides a "legitimate" excuse for offering advice, make the most of it!

So far I have used "Tips" as a sort of dessert—a pleasant morsel after the meat and potatoes portion of the chapter. Sometimes it's fun to have dessert first, and in this case, I think it may be necessary. So, let's start with a few tips, some of them about how to use this chapter.

Tip:

This chapter was placed here because it seemed a logical progression in terms of the age chronology we have been using in this book. But it contains bits of information about adult sexuality that are either supplements to or based on information given in Chapter Ten. You may, in fact, prefer to read the tenth chapter first, especially if your children are still young.

Tip:

Don't assume that your child is experienced just because statistics say he or she may be. It used to be that people would die before they'd admit experience; now they often feel reluctant about admitting lack of experience.

Tip:

Experience does not necessarily lead to knowledge. Many people have reached their twenty-fifth anniversary without much more understanding of how to have a good marital sexual relationship than how to get a penis into a vagina. There's lots more to a good sexual relationship than that. If your children are experienced, they may very well have even more questions and need more help than ever, especially since first attempts at intercourse are often very unsatisfactory. Open doors are just as important now as when they were younger.

Tip:

If you don't know how to broach the subject, especially the experience part, remember the old warmth, empathy and honesty, plus the "many people" concept. For example:

"You know, many people are pretty uncertain at first. I sure wished I'd had someone to answer my questions, so let's talk about some of the little things that come up."

"I'm feeling a bit awkward: I don't know if you want my help. I don't know what experience you've had, and I don't want to put you on the spot. But all people have some difficulties with sex at times, and I hope you'll feel free to be honest with me, so that we can talk about your real questions, not the ones I think you'll have."

"Now that you've had a chance to try things out, maybe you have some things you'd like to talk over. It'll be easier to answer questions now that you know what problems crop up."

If your children say they don't need your help, don't feel let down. Just keep the door open by letting them know you're available in the future, and feel free to open the door again yourself at some point.

Now let's get on to myths, some of which are about sex, and some of which are about love and marriage.

Myths about love

Many couples enter marriage or marriage-like relationships filled with myths about romantic love gleaned from novels, magazines, movies and stories spread by others. When their relationship, sexual and otherwise, does not live up to these romanticized ideas, the couple may feel that something is wrong. Take, for instance, that statement made in a popular novel and movie some years ago—"Love is never having to say you're sorry." With all due respect to the heroine, I am afraid that it was only her untimely death that kept their love so beautiful. A few more months of such an idiotic theory and the marriage would probably have been on the rocks.

With a few clues it's easy to recognize many of these myths. They are often found in captions under cartoons of cherubic creatures so sexless that they can appear naked in family magazines. They start with "Love is. . . ." "People who truly love each other. . . ." or "True love is . . . ."

Myth—True love is eternally constant and passionate.

Young couples should know that love is exciting and passionate part of the time, but that sometimes people feel merely pleasant toward those they love, and occasionally may feel neutrality, dislike and even hatred.

Myth—True love is wanting to be together all the time.

People in love enjoy each other's company part of the time, but sometimes they enjoy being apart. Some marriages, in fact, work only because the partners see each other fairly seldom, and when too much "togetherness" occurs, the marriage falls apart.

Myth—True love means never thinking about other people, especially members of the opposite sex in a sexual way.

No matter how much one loves one's partner, eventually one needs other people and friendships. One person can seldom fulfill all the needs of another. Sexually, one can be appreciative or even aroused by others without being disloyal. In fact, many a sexual relationship is enhanced because each partner is imagining a movie star or good-looking friends. Sexual fantasies about other people are extremely common, not disloyal.

Myth—True love means never having any secrets.

Honesty and openness are good, to be sure; but there are times when telling a partner about a fantasy or a past behavior will only hurt and will in no way help either of you. What good does it do to relieve one's sense of guilt if it only makes someone else unnecessarily miserable? Even where guilt is not involved, each person in even the closest of relationships is still an individual in his or her own right, and will need to reserve some corner of his or her mind for private unshared thoughts. Privacy of thought is perhaps the only right we can truly count on; it would be a shame for people to deliberately deprive themselves of it merely because of a romantic myth.

Myth—True love means always wanting sex at the same time, or at least always saying "yes" to the other person.

No matter how much people love each other, one person may not feel like having sex when the other one does, whether because of anger, fatigue, distractions, illness, or for no reason at all. We might hope that that person will say "yes" some of those times, in order to "give" in response to a loved one's needs. But no person should make a toy out of another person. Sex purely out of a sense of duty is usually not very satisfying to either person.

Myth—True love means having simultaneous orgasms.

Simultaneous orgasms can be fun. Marriage manuals used to place great stress on them, and many people worked terribly hard to have them. But they're difficult to achieve, and orgasm itself is such an intense self-involved physiological response, that during it one cannot possibly attend to the needs of another. Taking turns is fun too, and simultaneous orgasms need not be a goal.

Myth—True love means always having orgasms.

Orgasm is not an "always" event, and depends upon a variety of factors at any given point. Many men, in fact, show a definite decrease in ability to have orgasm as they become older, yet still enjoy sex very much. Many women love their partners very much, have a good sexual relationship, get a great deal of satisfaction from the warmth and intimacy of intercourse, yet reach orgasm only part of the time, occasionally, or never. Of course, orgasm is extremely pleasurable and tension relieving. If one or both partners are seldom or never having orgasm and would like to, there are many things the couple can do about it, and many ways in which counselling can help.

Myth—Oral sex is unnatural and not a part of love.

If one does not wish to engage in oral sex, one should not be forced to either give or receive it. But it can be extremely pleasurable either as a forerunner, an aftermath, or instead of intercourse, and can be very much a part of love.

Myth—True love means having orgasms through intercourse. In women it means vaginal orgasm through intercourse. Clitoral orgasm or orgasm via self, manual or oral stimulation is improper, unnatural and disloyal.

An orgasm is an orgasm. Who has the right to say how it should be obtained? Apparently a lot of people still have beliefs about how it should be done. Actually, the vagina has little, if any, sensation. Stroking the general clitoral area (not attacking it directly) or caressing a particular spot that a woman finds stimulating (many women prefer one side or another of the clitoris), is what produces the build-up of feelings that result in orgasm. Sensations from clitoral stimulation spread into the vagina through the contraction and relaxation of muscles. Intercourse by itself is often the least effective route to female orgasm, and women who don't realize this may think they are "frigid" when they are not. For both men and women, orgasm may be easier to reach via manual, oral, or self stimulation at any given time, and is perfectly "proper" "natural" and "loyal."

Myth—"Sex" always means "intercourse."

"Sex" is a general term that may mean merely cuddling, caressing, oral stimulation or self stimulation. A person may not feel like having intercourse, but be quite willing to have some form of sexual pleasure, or to give it to the other person.

Myth—People in love do not need vibrators, oils or any other sexual aids.

People who are hungry actually need only a few basic foods to satisfy their stomachs. But sometimes a little garnish on the salad, frosting on the cake, and a new recipe makes food more enjoyable. The same is true of sex "aids." Vibrators can also be very useful for women having trouble reaching orgasm, that is for stimulating the clitoris, not simulating intercourse. Sex aids do not usually replace the partner, nor are they insults to one's prowess. They are merely a little garnish to enhance physical pleasure, and in no way satisfy the need for warmth and affection that the relationship itself provides.

Myth—If two people truly love each other, they will not have sexual needs while one partner is away on a trip.

Sexuality is not something that is turned on and off at will. Sometimes the loneliness that occurs during absences actually increases the need for sexual gratification. Wanting it—or even getting it—need not be considered disloyal. Only the means of obtaining it may be a problem for some people.

People who love each other will never have an affair. Infidelity means the marriage is on the rocks.

Sometimes people who are "unfaithful" get physical gratification without any of the affection and caring that is part of the marriage. Sometimes it means that emotional needs are not being met in the marriage, the partner is seeking fulfillment elsewhere, and some counselling is in order. Some people have needs that just cannot be met in the marriage, and the other partner will have to decide whether he or she is willing to accept extra-marital activity. There are many reasons for infidelity, but it does not nec-- essarily mean a lack of love or that the marriage is a failure.

Lack of erection, premature ejaculation or lack of orgasm means that "someone" is frigid or impotent, "someone" is at fault and that that "someone" should get help.

"Frigid" and "impotent" are two of the most meaningless and hurtful words I know. Most men have occasional episodes of such problems, especially as they grow older, without it meaning a thing, and lack of orgasm during intercourse does not mean that a woman is incapable of sexual interest, pleasure or orgasm. If it's a continual problem, it may mean there are some roadblocks to be cleared away and new techniques to be tried. Only sometimes does it indicate marital or emotional problems. Nobody is to blame, no one need feel ashamed to seek professional help, the quickest route to solving the problem, and usually help is best given when both people are working on the solution.

True love means always being able to know or sense what the other person is thinking, feeling or wanting.

Often people who have been married a long time or those who know each other very well develop the ability to respond fairly accurately to many non-verbal cues. But that does not make them mind readers, and even that ability comes from a result of good verbal communication. You can help your children tremendously by helping them realize that the sooner they start being honest with each other about what they like and dislike, communicating their needs clearly, the easier it will be. Communication is one of the most important things they will have to learn, in or out of bed.

TIPS THAT PARENTS OFTEN FORGET TO GIVE

Sex can be messy.

Many women expect to enter and leave the bed with themselves and the bed clean, unmussed and dry. After all, that's the way it is in the movies. Faced with an unexpected need for a box of tissues, they feel "dirty" and may think something is wrong. They worry about protocol. Should they lie in bed and suffer, lie in bed and enjoy it, stroll or rush to the bathroom? They should know ahead of time that a box of tissues by the bed can come in handy, that the amount of "messiness" will vary from time to time, that women differ in their reactions, and that anything they wish to do at any given point is "okay."

A little lubrication can make a big difference, especially for people who are inexperienced and/or tense.

Some people think that because vaginal lubrication is one sign of sexual excitement and readiness for penile penetration, lack of lubrication means the woman is not excited, and that artificial lubrication is "cheating." Some women lubricate less than others, or may have had less lubrication because of recent use of tampons. Sometimes the stroking that is meant to excite eventually takes away lubrication, and becomes physically irritating instead of exciting. No matter what the reason, artificial lubrication can both enhance the sensations that lead to natural lubrication, and can enable penetration to take place more easily. It is neither cheating nor disloyal.

Menstruation on the wedding day is a common experience.

Unless there is a religious, esthetic or personal reason for abstaining, menstruation need not interfere with intercourse. But for those who would choose to abstain, body stroking, oral sex, petting to orgasm, are ways of getting to know what pleases the other person, and may be the best thing that ever happened to them in terms of long range goals.

If one or both partners are inexperienced or tense, penetration may be difficult or impossible at first.

Couples who don't know this feel inadequate, angry, disappointed and more tense the next time they try. A man who decides to go full steam ahead on the theory that "once he gets it in, she'll love it," is causing needless discomfort. It may sound great in the pornography books, but painful, forced intercourse does not endear women to the prospect of future lovemaking. The tension that results can create even more pain and much mutual dissatisfaction. Better to try out other ways of gratification while easing gradually into intercourse. If they don't succeed within a few weeks, the couple should certainly get professional help without further ado.

Men need not always be the aggressor, and should not be held totally responsible for the woman's enjoyment.

Women are not meant to be passive during sexual activity, they are meant to have fun!

There is no "right" way, time or place to have sex.

While a good sexual relationship is not instinctive and often takes a lot of time—sometimes years—to truly achieve, that time should be spent having fun, not "working." Many people approach sex as if it were a job that must be handled quickly, efficiently and correctly. They worry about what is "right" and "wrong," and cannot understand it when they think they've followed the rules and have still not reached their goal. You can do a lot to help your children by helping them realize that by using honesty, warmth and empathy plus a good sense of humor, they can learn what is enjoyable for them, and that is all that's necessary.

Along with the "work" orientation toward sex goes another idea that interferes with pleasure by creating tension. Many people approach each "work" session as a life or death matter in which they either prove their adequacy or doom themselves forever. I have, to be sure, suggested that sex is important in people's lives. Yet therapists find that the last, seemingly contradictory, tip is very helpful even to people who are extremely upset about sexual problems. That tip is:

In any single act of lovemaking, the specific act of sex in itself is not really such a big deal! If it doesn't work out right one time, it will another!

CHAPTER TEN

QUESTIONS ADULTS ASK ABOUT SEX

Much of the following material will be about adult sexuality. Some information will be on topics that you may never need to, wish to, or even be allowed the chance to discuss with your children. So why is it important to know or to put in a book of this kind?

There are three main reasons. First, the more you know , the more prepared you are for the unexpected question or situation and the more helpful you can be to your children when they become adults. Second, it's difficult to deal adequately with children about sex if you have not come to grips with adult sexuality, and particularly with your own. It's hard to talk easily about homosexuality with a troubled teenager, for instance, if your stomach turns over the minute you hear that word. It's hard to know how to deal with or discuss masturbation with a child if you're not sure whether it's harmful or helpful, and are perhaps feeling a little uncertain about your own sexual behavior or adequacy, (and who doesn't at times?). Futhermore you may fear you will be vulnerable to criticism, should "opening doors" ever lead to another's knowledge about what you do in private. While comfort about your own sexuality is not something you can get just from reading a book, knowing that much of what you go through is shared by others, and knowing some facts can help a lot.

We all have questions about sex and keep a ready eye and ear open for tips on how to enhance our own sexual relationships. So this is a bonus reason—even though it may not be the actual purpose you or I had in mind, the more you know the more apt you are to apply such tips to your own life, and that in itself can indirectly help you help your children. The following will not deal with all of the questions people have about sex, and you may well want to follow with additional reading or perhaps a course. But it will include some of the most common concerns that people seem to have. Let's start with the most basic—and possibly most difficult—question to answer:

What is sex?

When people use the word "sex," it is actually difficult to know what they really mean, for the word means many different things to people. Forced to give a quick definition, most people seem to say "intercourse." It encompasses so much more that a single definition is not adequate. My husband, Harvey, who teaches human sexuality at the University of Hawaii, sees sex as having six interrelated aspects: Reproduction, sensuality, intimacy, sexualization, attitudes and emotions, identity and object choice.

Reproduction

This is the area with which we are probably most familiar, and which until recently has been the focus of most of our formal sex education. It includes the biological processes that enable us to reproduce (menstrual cycle), the actual behavior leading to reproduction (sexual intercourse), and the natural biological consequences of that behavior (pregnancy). It also includes our attitudes toward those processes and goes beyond to childbirth, children, parenthood, and ourselves as real or potential parents.

Sensuality

Sensuality is the giving and receiving of pleasurable sensations via the body. It may involve such senses as smell, taste or hearing, but most often we think of it in terms of touch, via the skin. Many children and adults enjoy feeling soft velvet, squishing toes in sandy lake bottoms, being caressed or stroked gently, or being given massages and back rubs; thus, we are responding to the sensuality of our daily encounters.

Sensuality may or may not, then, have to do with intercourse, although it's often an important part of lovemaking that's come to be known as "foreplay." New mothers sometimes find themselves aroused even to orgasm while nursing their infants. That doesn't mean they're turned on to babies—it merely means that an area of their bodies especially sensitive to touch has responded to sensual stimulation. One wonders if nature designed things that way so that infants of all species would get fed.

When we talk about "childhood sexuality," apart from the child's natural curiosity about everything, including human bodies and behavior, we are really talking about sensuality. Children are extremely sensual creatures. They have been known to masturbate during infancy, some babies even showing the facial expressions usually associated with adult orgasm. They suck their thumbs, nuzzle and rub their blankets and sheets, adore their mothers' fur coats, caress and enjoy being caressed, and derive their sense of well being from some form of sensual contact (for an example, note the security blanket). They engage in such social sexual relationships as "playing doctor" games—partly because of curiosity but also because it is fun, and may feel good in a sensual way. When they grow up they bring those same needs into adult sexual expression, adding kissing, oral-genital contact, intercourse, and so on, to their repertoire of sexual behavior.

Here is an experiment you can do:

Close your eyes, hold out your bare arm, and lightly stroke it with the finger tips of your other hand. Does it feel reasonably pleasant? That is sensuality. It does not necessarily make you head for the nearest bedroom or provoke any sense of guilt, and has nothing to do with intercourse. Yet some forms of sensuality can be immensely pleasurable, even producing orgasm, all by themselves. Sex therapists will sometimes tell their patients to have sex every night. They do not mean intercourse—they mean caressing, stroking, expressing affection in some sensual way that may or may not lead to intercourse.

Identity and object choice

Identity refers to gender: the attributes that identify us (or others) as male or female, and often the roles we identify with that gender. Object choice means who or perhaps what we choose to use as a sexual partner. Usually our object choice is a person of the opposite gender, but it may be of the same gender, it may be ourselves, and it may vary from time to time. Some people use animals or clothing. Percentage-wise these last choices are few, but even the lowest possible percentage of the total population can include an extremely large number of people.

Intimacy

Intimacy is often confused with sex, probably because it is a very important part of sex. It includes love and affection, but more importantly it includes the ability to share with someone private thoughts that we are unwilling to share with others, allowing us to be vulnerable with another person with some assurance that we will not be hurt as a result. As much trouble as we seem to have with sexuality, we seem to have even more with intimacy. We are hesitant to risk being laughed at, rejected, or hurt in any way and yet, we very much need the closeness and warmth that affection and intimacy brings. Often we confuse sexual intercourse with intimacy, and many people will engage in sexual behavior not out of desire, but because they're hoping to find intimacy. Conversely, some people think that if they are emotionally intimate with someone, sexual intercourse is an expected consequence. It's important to realize that one can have sex without intimacy and intimacy without sex. The one does not necessarily include or lead to the other. I'll probably use this word often, because it's so important to people.

Sexualization

Sexualization is the use of sex to fulfill needs that are not actually sexual. We may use it to gain money, power, love, intimacy, or to relieve general tension, loneliness, fear, or to express anger. It can be used to get someone to do something in particular for us. An advertiser may use it to sell cars. A child may use it to get attention. A movie star may use it to get a good role. A person may use it to get a spouse to pay attention to him or her. Sometimes "sexualization" can be helpful. A couple, for instance, might have a huge fight and then make up, affirming their love for each other through intercourse. However, that same act can be harmful if one or both partners are using it to express their anger, if one is using it to assert his or her dominance, or if it is being used to cover up and avoid problems that need to be worked out. Sometimes sexualization can be exploitative, using another person for one's own needs, without any concern for that person's needs. A common example is that of a man dating a woman in whom he has no interest, but whose sexiness brings him prestige. He may insist that she have intercourse with him to reaffirm his own masculinity and adequacy without regards for her needs. Men do not have a corner on this problem, women can be exploitive and often are.

Some thoughts on the sexual revolution

Many authorities on sex feel that the so-called sexual revolution is merely a dramatic highlighting of gradual changes in our perceptions of the various aspects of sex. The changes in behavior that we see are the result of increasing separation between the reproductive functions of sex and its other aspects.

In the past, the stability of a culture, religion, nation, or family depended on its ability to produce healthy children. Overpopulation has begun to decrease the need for so many babies. As we have begun to develop effective means of contraception to control birth rates, society has begun to pay greater attention to such functions of sex as providing intimacy, tension release, recreation and sensual pleasure, and to see reproduction as only one of many of our sexual functions.

Accordingly, this has opened more options for many people who either cannot produce or take care of children, or who may not wish to produce children at a certain time. The sexual revolution and the women's movement have increasingly recognized women as having sexual needs and rights apart from their childbearing function. Now attitudes are beginning to change concerning the sexual needs and rights of people such as the retarded, the aged, the physically handicapped, the dying, the homosexually oriented person, and the institutionalized person, even though such people might not wish or be able to have children. (Gochros and Gochros, 1972).

Sexual activity apart from marriage, as well as behaviors that do not lead to pregnancy, such as masturbation, oral sex, and caressing to orgasm are becoming increasingly more acceptable. Society has also begun to reevaluate ideas about morality and responsibility, and to redefine concepts of "masculinity" and "femininity." In doing so, people have begun to worry less about narrow concepts of "right" and "wrong," or "normal" versus "abnormal," to think more about what the consequences of any act might be for the people involved, and to allow themselves pleasurable behavior with or without a reproductive goal in mind.

This has been termed a separation between the "work" and

"play" functions of sex, with greater acceptance of those who either cannot work or who at some point wish only to play.

Many people wonder if this means our society is becoming immoral, promiscuous, and irresponsible. That's impossible to answer, since each person defines such terms differently. But it may comfort you to know that while there are profound changes in sexual behavior, things have still not changed as much as it might seem.

Morton Hunt, who has conducted perhaps the most extensive research since Kinsey's famous study, found that while there is more sex outside of marriage—especially for women—than there used to be, it is not indiscriminate sex. People are not hopping into bed with anybody and everybody; they still prefer sex in a loving and meaningful relationship far more than sex purely for physical release.

The so-called revolution is an attempt to solve some of the problems of past generations: hypocrisy (in which we often did secretly what we are now doing more honestly), unhappiness, fear, ignorance, game playing, and exploitation. It is an effort to create *more* honesty, responsibility and morality, not less. Whether it will succeed in that, of course, still remains to be seen.

Is the younger generation free of hangups and problems then? Definitely not! Any solution to a problem creates its own problems, which in turn require new solutions. It is those new problems with which your children will need more help than ever, for in some ways they are even more difficult than the old ones. For example, we used to have strict rules about sexual behavior. We all knew what they were. We only had two choices, to obey them or not. Now the rules are fuzzier. For many, there are fewer absolutes about right and wrong. Our children will have to decide for themselves in each situation which behaviors are acceptable.

Being the decision maker and being responsible for your actions isn't always easy. Our children will need us to provide them with values and will need our help in making their decisions in the light of those values.

Here are some more problems which changing attitudes create. Sometimes in the search for love and intimacy in a cold world people mistake sex for love. In the name of "freedom" (the *name* is sometimes changed without changing the *game*) people are made to feel "abnormal" if they don't choose to be liberated. "What do you mean you won't have intercourse with me? I thought you were liberated!" is a common expression today of yesterday's theme, exploitation and conformity. It isn't love, liberation, consideration, or responsibility at all. It leaves young people just as confused, vulnerable, lonely, and frightened as ever.

Some consequences of premarital sex are less severe than they used to be. There is not as much criticism and public scorn to fear. Also, with contraceptives, one has less fear of pregnancy. But other problems such as venereal disease and abortion are on the rise. This is partly because young people are afraid to ask their partners to help prevent such problems. They may then face just as serious emotional and moral struggles as ever.

To pretend we have *the answer* to the many problems in the sexual revolution is ridiculous and self-defeating. Our children know we don't. What we can do, is try our hardest to help them make the revolution succeed in its effort to allow for sex that is both recreational and responsible for everyone.

COMMON SEXUAL BEHAVIORS

Let's go on to some of the more common sexual behaviors, starting with the one that is by far the most common one of all, and try to answer some of the questions people seem to have. Most people are surprised to learn that that behavior is not intercourse.

Masturbation

Often called self-stimulation, the handling or stimulation of one's own genitals to produce sensual pleasure—often to orgasm— is probably one of the earliest and most common forms of sexual behavior. Despite the fact that over ninety two per cent of adult American men, and anywhere from fifty to eighty per cent of women masturbate at some time or another—and I suspect that eventually the statistics on women will approximate those on men— it's still viewed with an amazing amount of fear and confusion. When teenagers call up anonymously to ask questions about sex, masturbation is one of their most frequent concerns. So here are some of the questions I'm asked most often: *Is it common? Who does it? How often? At what age? And why?*

As you can see from the above statistics, it's certainly a common activity, that may start in infancy and continue till the day a person dies. We may think of it as a teenage sexual activity, but children, adults, singles, married couples, and elderly people also engage in it.

Teenagers probably masturbate most often—sometimes several times a day—for they have the greatest sexual needs and fewer other outlets. It is common for people to stimulate themselves at least once a day, once a week, once a year, or less often, depending upon individual circumstances. Some people never do it, but they are in the minority. The reasons people stimulate themselves are simple: it feels good and it relieves tension of all kinds, both physical and emotional.

Many women do not realize that it's almost as common for them as it is for men, although our statistics are not as clear for females as they are for males. That is partly because women have been taught that they should not have sexual feelings, and consequently are more hesitant both about masturbating and reporting it. They may also feel more guilty about it because it sometimes involves putting the fingers into the vagina, and they've been taught that is wrong. Finally, in some women, it merely involves tightening one's muscles or pressing one's legs together, perhaps in the process of engaging in another non-sexual activity. Such activity may stimulate the clitoris enough to produce a pleasant sensation or some tension relief, but not be enough to produce the strong sensations which women experience as sexual ones. Hence they do not perceive themselves as masturbating, and do not get reported in the statistics.

Are fantasies while masturbating harmful?

Sexual fantasies are common during masturbation, intercourse, or any other sexual behavior. In fantasy one can do all the forbidden and therefore exciting things that one might not be able to do—and might not want to do—in real life. Moreover, fantasies keep one from becoming overly preoccupied with the mechanics of sex. They are usually so helpful that therapists will often encourage their use, in conjunction with masturbation, as a step toward developing more satisfactory sexual relationships. These techniques teach people how to enhance their everyday fantasy life.

Sexual fantasies are unlikely to be harmful, unless a person is able to become aroused only by fantasies of such antisocial behavior as child molestation. In that case, the person can try to teach him or herself to enjoy fantasies which would be more socially acceptable, such as sex with peers. If a person is unable to do so, he or she might seek assistance from a sex counsellor. Such a problem is not common, so generally speaking, you need not worry about fantasies. Enjoy them, and remember, you don't have to act on them.

Is too much masturbation a sign of emotional problems or of being oversexed?

How does one define "oversexed" or "too much?" Is three times a week "okay" and four times "too much?" We tend to worry too much about numbers.

If someone is masturbating to the exclusion of all other activities or even of sex that he or she would prefer having with an available partner, then we might suspect that this is trying to relieve not sexual tension, but worry, fear, boredom, or anger, and that it is not succeeding. In that case, we would probably want to help with those problems, but such extremes are not very common. Small children may fondle themselves several times a day, often absent mindedly, without it meaning anything. Teenagers, whose major job in life is learning to cope with emerging sexual feelings, spend a lot of time each day in fantasy and masturbation. Adults, who may have other options open to them, probably do it less, but they too may do it once or several times a day. Only if it interferes with other functions of daily life without relieving the tension it was meant to relieve, is it a problem to worry about.

Why would married people do it? Is something wrong with the marriage?

If self stimulation is being used to avoid sex with the partner or because one or both partners are continually dissatisfied, we might suspect that there are problems at least in the sexual part of the marriage, and perhaps in other parts as well. However, that usually is not the case. Sometimes one partner has greater sexual needs than the other, or has them at a time when the other one doesn't. Sometimes one may be away, sick, having a period, or has just delivered a baby. Occasionlly, even the greatest lovers will have an unsuccessful experience with intercourse, with one or both partners left unsatisfied. Often watching one partner stimulate him or herself, or doing it to the other person, is an exciting prelude to intercourse. Sometimes both partners want the tension release of orgasm plus the intimacy of the relationship, yet do not feel like having intercourse. Also, because many women can have multiple orgasms, a woman might have an orgasm and still feel the need for "just a little more." She really doesn't want more intercourse, and anyhow, her husband is possibly already asleep. Many women stimulate themselves at such times; masturbation eases the physical tension and provides satisfaction. In fact, having such an option can improve ability to have satisfying intercourse. When people know that they can both satisfy and be satisfied with or without intercourse, it eases the sense of "responsibility" for another person, and the worry and preoccupation that so often interferes with pleasurable intercourse.

Yes, but shouldn't adults have a little more self control and discipline about sexual needs?

Haven't you ever had a good, satisfying meal and yet felt like a little snack a few hours later? Or even an after dinner mint? Do you berate yourself for being immoral or undisciplined? Probably only if your snacking becomes a problem and you begin gaining unwanted pounds or become so satiated that you can't enjoy the steak dinner you would like to have with your partner. Only then do you decide to control your behavior. Until that happens, the snacks you have, maybe two or three times a day, provide not only food, but pleasure and relaxation that may indeed enable you to function more efficiently. They help, not hurt you. The same can be said of self-stimulation, and according to research, with possibly less chance of becoming overfull.

Are you saying then that masturbation should be encouraged?

Most people do not need encouragement. There are times, however, when it might be useful or even necessary to provide both information and encouragement, for this activity certainly has some beneficial results. For all it may give temporary relief from loneliness, fear or worry, and for people having difficulty achieving satisfaction through intercourse, it is often a beginning step in giving help.

It is good preparation for intercourse; adolescent boys who practice controlling ejaculation during masturbation are more apt to learn to control it long enough to satisfy their partners. Girls who experience orgasm before marriage are more apt to experience orgasm in marriage. Also, the more people learn about their own bodies and what pleases them, the more able they will be to help their partners know how to please them.

For those who are permanently or temporarily without a partner—for example, teenagers, military personnel, or other traveling people and their spouses, widows and widowers, or single persons of any age—self stimulation may be a far more acceptable outlet than intercourse. For many people, such as the retarded, handicapped, sick, or dying it may be the only outlet available.

Masturbation might be the most effective tranquilizer we could find; it is always available, free, can be enjoyed with or without another person, and usually has no side effects. So unless there is a particular reason to discourage it, I'd either not worry about it or I might even actively encourage some use of it.

What do I do if either I or my church considers masturbation immoral?

You cannot accept these ideas if they conflict with doctrines which are important to you. You need apologize to no one for your beliefs and you should share them with your children.

You should know two things, however. First, people whose religion forbids it still do it. They may feel more guilty about it than others not inhibited by religious doctrines; according to both Kinsey and Hunt, they may use it less often than others do especially if very devout. But generally speaking, masturbation is a common practice for people, no matter what their religion or religious beliefs.

The second thing you should know is that many churches have changed their attitudes toward it. Even where an official change has not yet taken place, interpretation of church law may differ from minister to minister, or priest to priest. Check with several of your religious leaders whether priest, minister, rabbi, or guru, and you may find them more accepting than you think. (Although that does not mean *you* have to change *your* mind). Also, I have heard some leaders of even the most traditionally oriented churches say to their parishioners, "Don't feel too guilty if you give in to the impulse once in a while, and tell the same to your child. God doesn't expect us to be perfect—He only expects us to try."

Tip:

Be honest with your children about your own values and your reasons for them. Don't apologize or vacillate. Also be honest about the fact that others may disagree, for in the end the children will have to decide for themselves. Not only will they respect you for it, but they'll probably be more receptive to your thinking.

Is masturbation normal?

If "normal" means "common," then there's no question that it is a common experience. I do not use "normal" to define "common." Since being "normal" seems to worry many people, and since it will come up with every other sexual behavior, let's stop a minute and think about it.

"Normal" is a source of great confusion to people, probably because it conveys two meanings: one means "typical," "common," or "usual"; the other is a psychological term which may under certain circumstances, mean "free from any mental disorder." When we use this term (or its antonym, "abnormal") we often get the two kinds of meanings confused. The first meaning merely states a numerical or class fact, while the second makes a value judgment, implying that deviation from the norm is bad, wrong, or sick. The second meaning is a relative judgment that may change from time to time or place to place. As an example, bare legs might be both common and normal in our country, while they might be both unusual and immoral in India, or unusual but normal in another country.

That sort of labeling often interferes with others' rights or our own ability to satisfy our own needs, and actually makes no sense. *If many do it, is it right? If few do it, is it wrong?* We know better than to get caught up in such a dilemma in other areas, for we often tell our children, "I don't care how many other children stay up until eleven, you may not." Or "Don't follow the herd; use your own judgment."

In teaching, I try to avoid the words "normal" or "abnormal." It is, I must admit, difficult to avoid words that are so often used. I try to get around it by using the word "common" and "uncommon," and by discussing the advantages and problems associated with any behavior. Then students have a better framework than my bias on which to guide their thinking.

Masturbation, then, is neither "normal" or "abnormal." It exists, and it is an extremely common sexual behavior. Whether it is good, bad, moral, immoral, or a sign of emotional health or disturbance will depend on the person and the situation.

Is anything acceptable then? Are there no rules?

Of course there must be rules! Not everything is acceptable. Some behaviors, like constant open masturbation intrude on the normal functioning of everyday life, and may, for a given individual, be a symptom of emotional disturbance that should be discouraged and for which counselling should be sought.

Ground rules for masturbation should be:

It should supplement, not supplant other daily activities.

It should be done in private surroundings.

It should never be done with sharp, dangerous objects.

Ground rules for any sexual behavior which involves another person should be:

> It should be done in privacy, only with a person who is completely willing. It should only be done if both people are either responsible adults or children of approximately the same age, strength, and mental competence.
>
> It should only be done if it will help, not hurt one or both of the people involved. "Hurting" means more than causing physical pain. It includes exploiting or using someone, causing guilt in someone who considers it immoral, getting someone in trouble with parents or other authorities, and "emotionally" forcing or socially pressuring someone.

Knowledge can make a difference in how comfortably and sensitively you deal with your children. A mother I know reported realizing, after a workshop discussion on masturbation, that she had been needlessly worrying about her teenage son. One day she forgot to knock, and realized from the panicky look on his face what he had been doing. Instead of panicking herself, as she might have done earlier, she merely said, "Gee, I'm sorry! I didn't realize you were busy," and quickly closed his bedroom door and left. Later he told her how reassuring her comment had been, that he had been feeling guilty about masturbation, and had questions that he'd hesitated to ask.

Masturbation, then, like most other sexual behaviors, should be viewed in the context of whether it is helpful or harmful to a given person at a given time and place.

Intercourse and orgasm

We've actually covered many of the questions often asked about intercourse and orgasm in the previous chapter. If you'll take a quick review, you'll see that many of them have "Am I normal" as an underlying theme. Is there a right way to have intercourse? Is it "normal" to need artificial lubrication? Here are some more.

How often should people have intercourse?

Again there are many statistics on how often people tend to have intercourse at different ages, but statistics do not take into account individual needs. Younger couples tend to have it more often, but some enjoy it daily (or more often) others weekly, others once a month, and still others less often.

I once knew a couple who had intercourse only once a year on Christmas Eve. According to every textbook around, this couple should have been having severe problems. Yet their communication with and concern for each other enabled them to enjoy that one night tremendously and they were very happy together.

Another couple came for counselling because they were enjoying sex less and fighting more. It turned out that the stories they'd heard and the statistics they'd read had convinced them that they were abnormal because they were not having intercourse as often as others seemed to. Consequently they were having it when neither one wanted it, and the result was not enjoyment but worry, frustration, and anger. When given "permission" to be themselves, their earlier enjoyment of each other both as marital and sexual partners returned.

What are the differences between male and female sexual responses and needs? Are men "sexier" than women?

This is difficult to answer well, because while there are differences between men and women, we are becoming increasingly aware that many of those differences are cultural and learned, rather than innate. More and more we are seeing that women have much the same needs and capabilities as men.

Men do seem to show an earlier, stronger sex drive, and during their teens, are capable of almost instant erections, with four to eight orgasms a day not unusual, either through intercourse, masturbation, or nocturnal emissions. A friend recently told me that his memory of adolescence was of "one constant erection", an agonizing experience because he was so constantly worried about whether other people would notice. Other men in group discussion report similar experiences. By the time they reach thirty, their sense of urgency is less acute, they are satisfied with fewer orgasms, and by the age of fifty, may be having two orgasms a week or less. Women seem to show more individual variation, do not seem to have the same sense of urgency, and reach their peak later, often having more orgasms during their thirties, forties and later than they did in their twenties.

Men may respond more quickly to visual stimuli, and at least while younger, their arousal is an intense genitally centered sensation. For women, arousal is more a generalized, total body experience, and more often connected with emotional attachment. Hence, they seem to enjoy more total body stroking than men do, with a gradual buildup of sexual excitement.

But again, newer research may invalidate some of these differences. We are already finding indications that women do respond to visual stimulation and that such behavior as sexual assertiveness (formerly a male perogative) is becoming more common. With proper stimulation, many women are both capable of multiple orgasms and very immediate ones. Men too may find total body stroking both stimulating and pleasurable, may find stimulation of the nipples highly exciting, may sometimes have multiple orgasms, or no orgasm at all. We are just beginning to realize how much we do not know yet, especially about female sexuality, and as female needs are more accepted, their behaviors are apt to change.

How does aging affect sexuality?

People can enjoy sex even in their eighties—sometimes beyond. Many people do not realize this. They misinterpret the word "peak" so often found in the literature about sex, and visualize a pinnacle like a mountain peak that occurs at a specific age, and from which there is a plummeting downward to the bottom. In actuality, there is no exact "peak," but rather a leveling off and descent that is so gradual that it may be hardly noticeable. Even the more noticeable changes that menopause brings for women, and that occur for men of a similar age range, may be gradual, starting long before a person considers herself or himself middle aged. Youth, middle age, and old age, then, are not so sharply separated that we know when one ends and the other begins. The changes that aging brings to sex are as continual, gradual, and variable as they are for any functions of the body. It is probably a slower process for the genitalia than for any other part of the human body.

There are, nevertheless, changes that must be increasingly taken into account as people become older. Men may become aroused less quickly, and their erections may be at a lower angle, less firm, more quickly lost following intercourse. There may be fewer orgasms and less amount of ejaculation. Women, because of the gradual thinning of the vaginal lining (particularly after menopause) may have less lubrication and may need more artificial lubrication or possibly hormonal treatment in order to avoid irritation or pain. Both men and women may find intercourse too fatiguing at night, and may prefer the morning or daytime hours. These differences are not necessarily problems. They may require new techniques, a bit of understanding and humor, and good communication.

Recently I heard about a thirty year old woman who was propositioned by an eighty year old man. Asked later why she would be interested in him, she replied, "Well, not only was he charming and attentive, he told me that he would adore making love to me if I'd be willing to meet him at 8:00 A.M. , since that was the only time he could be sure of "getting it up." With such refreshing candor, how could I refuse?"

Unfortunately, many men have difficulty with erection once or twice, think they've "had it," and are afraid to try again. Their female partners may not realize that this is part of the aging process, and think they've lost their sexual attractiveness. Also, many women think that menopause or a hysterectomy spells the end of sexual desire, attractiveness, or ability. Not only do the changes in aging not spell disaster, they may be quite helpful. Feeling less need for ejaculation, older men find it easier to retain erections during intercourse long enough to attend to female needs. Freed from the worries of pregnancy, child care, and chores, many women experience a greater desire and pleasure than they ever had while younger.

The illnesses that often occur in old age may require special attention. But generally, if people recognize that "sex" encompasses far more than intercourse and reproduction, and includes masturbation, general caressing, affection, and intimacy, aging can provide the best of sexual relationships.

What is an orgasm? How do I know if I've had one? And how do I talk to my children about it?

Orgasm, like taste, is difficult to describe especially for women who do not have an ejaculation to aid in the explanation.
Primarily it's a sudden release of tension, such as when the air is let out of a balloon. It is such an intense, physiological response that during it, the person is totally immersed in his or her own body sensations, and is oblivious to others.

There has never been a description that is completely satisfying. Some people have described it as akin to a sneeze. I consider it more akin to sensations felt when engaging in a good long "stretch," or even of a less esthetic experience—the tremendous relief one feels when emptying a very full bladder. It generally is followed by body relaxation, a sense of emotional well being, and pleasure.

Male orgasms have two components: tension release and e-jaculation. Women, despite heavy lubrication, have no equivalent of ejaculation. The process of reaching, achieving, and ending orgasm is less complex and variable for men than it is for women. For that reason, we will be focusing here mostly on female orgasm, though generally, the comments made here will apply to men.

Once it became acknowledged that sex is pleasurable— even for women— we began to oversell. Asked by children what intercourse or orgasm feels like, many adults say things like "It's the most beautiful feeling you ever had" or (in a mysterious, knowing voice) "It's fantastic! I can't describe it, but when you have one, you'll know it!" Such high expectations can lead to frustration and disappointment.

For both men and women, orgasms range in quantity and quality from minor bits of tension release that temporarily reduce sexual excitement, to very intense body sensations that produce complete body relaxation afterwards. Many women think that they've never had a "real" orgasm, merely because no bombs burst and no bells rang. But while some orgasms are "ecstasy," more are merely "pleasant" or "nice," some are even just "okay." Occasionally it merely releases enough tension to provide a "resting point" during which a woman will need more caressing in order to stimulate her to a more intense orgasm.

Tip:

Often people are not aware of those resting points, sometimes called "plateaus", and limit their stroking to "foreplay"; many women need continued stroking throughout orgasm.

Tip:

Although there has been considerable discussion recently about the importance of the clitoris in female sexuality, many people still do not know how to effectively stimulate it. Although in structure, it is the equivalent of the penis (other than that it is not used for urination and has only one function—that of producing pleasure), it is small in area and as sensitive as the head of the penis. Hence, the long, firm stroking that many men enjoy may be unpleasant or even painful, and the fraction of an inch or the slightest variation in touch may make a big difference in enjoyment. Many women find that stroking one side of the clitoral area is more pleasurable than the other, or that after a certain amount of arousal, they no longer enjoy stimulation of the clitoral area. Physical response is so varied from woman to woman or moment to moment, that women will do well here to experiment by themselves as well as with their partner, and to be clear about their wishes at a given moment.

Tip:

When asked by children what orgasm or intercourse feels like, also try to avoid under-selling. You won't fool them or prevent premarital sex by denying that sex is fun; you may merely increase their disappointment when a marriage license fails to remove the inhibitions you deliberately created.

Another tip:

Avoid telling them "You'll understand when you're older." They can understand your difficulty in explanations about such feelings as orgasm or sexual arousal if you compare it to trying to describe a taste or emotion. You will appear honest, instead of evasive.

What are some of the common problems in intercourse?

The most common problems for men are difficulty in obtaining or maintaining an erection, and having orgasm and ejaculation too early to allow the woman to be satisfied. The most common problems for women are pain and difficulty in achieving orgasm.

While people experiencing problems should certainly be checked by a doctor, usually the problem is merely that they're trying too hard to reach a predetermined goal (usually orgasm) and are so worried about failure that they're forgetting to relax and enjoy themselves. Such problems are often complicated by poor communication, in which one or both partners are afraid to really tell the other what he or she really wants, plus feelings of anger, self blame, rejection, and inadequacy.

The solutions? The problems of erection maintenance and achieving orgasm often respond to more experimentation, different forms of gratification such as oral and manual stimulation and better communication assisted by a generous share of warmth, honesty, empathy, and humor. For vaginal pain upon entrance, sometimes added lubrication is all that is needed, or merely a change of positions for pain during intercourse. If this doesn't work quickly, a physician should certainly be consulted to make sure that nothing is medically wrong.

If none of these solutions seem to work, counselling is in order. It may be that other marital or psychological problems are interfering. Also, sexual problems alone, left to snowball, can eventually interfere with even a basically sound marriage. A trained counsellor will be able to help pinpoint the problems and assist in reaching solutions.

Oral sex

Oral sex means stimulation of the genitals by the tongue or lips. When a woman kisses, licks, or takes the penis into her mouth, it is called *fellatio,* and when the man kisses, licks, or inserts his tongue into the vagina or around the clitoral area, it is called *cunnilingus.* Many people feel this is dirty or abnormal, but unless one partner has an infection, (particularly a venereal one), in his or her mouth, or anal intercourse was used first without washing the penis, there's no reason to worry. You may be surprised to hear how common an activity it is. In 1974, Morton Hunt found that over half of the total adults studied had engaged in both forms of it (although blacks, for various reasons, used it less than whites). Of the married couples studied, four-fifths of the college educated couples under the age of thirty-five and nine-tenths of *all* couples under the age of twenty-five had engaged in it. Here are some of the questions people ask about it:

Why do people do it? What are the advantages and disadvantages?

It's extremely pleasurable, because tongues are just lighter and moister than hands. It may produce orgasms much more quickly and intensely than either manual stimulation or intercourse. It is less likely than intercourse to spread venereal disease, and of course, it never produces babies. Problems, then, are mainly psychological; some women do not like the idea of receiving the ejaculate in their mouths. If a woman does not wish to overcome this, or cannot, it should be respected. Some women are unable to take the full penis into their mouths, and this should be respected. Some people find oral sex unenjoyable or even downright distasteful, do not wish to even try it, and this too should be respected.

You may never need to, or wish to, or be allowed to talk with your children about it. But many children ask, and you may actually want your teenagers to know that it is one way to have sexual pleasure without fear of pregnancy. So don't be afraid to talk about it, or even to say that you engage in it if you do. Your children may say "Yuck" to it, but they say "Yuck" to intercourse too, at first. You can just use the empathy ("It does sound pretty strange, doesn't it!") and the "many people" concept ("But though it's hard to explain, many, many people do it"). That they will try it out eventually, whether or not you talk about it, seems to be a statistically safe prediction.

Anal sex

Anal sex may be merely stimulation of the anal area or it may mean actual insertion of the penis or fingers into the anal opening. It is much less common than any of the other activities we've mentioned, and is used more for an occasional bit of experimentation in marriage than as a regular form of sexual gratification, (although homosexual males use it more often than heterosexuals do). Nevertheless, from eleven to thirteen percent of married couples in Hunt's studies, over the age of thirty-five, and well over half of those under the age of thirty-five had engaged in anal sex at some time or another. It seems to be an increasingly common behavior.

The advantages are that many people find it stimulating and pleasurable. Disadvantages are partly that many people find the idea distasteful; but apart from that, there is greater chance for infection, and unless each partner is extremely sensitive to the others needs, and extremely gentle, tense muscles could make it either painful or injurious to delicate tissues. But, of course, that's also true, to some degree, of intercourse. Again, the main ground rules are respect and good communication. If one goes immediately to or from anal intercourse to either vaginal or oral sex, the genital areas should be washed throughly first, to prevent any possible spread of bacteria.

Summing up the various sexual behaviors we have mentioned, let's remember that sexual response is highly individual and varies widely from person to person and from moment to moment. Anything that is acceptable and pleasurable to the parties involved is "all right," whether it is a question of which position to use, what time or place, how often, or what "garnishes" are used (music, lights, oils, etc.).

LIVING TOGETHER AND OPEN MARRIAGE

As our society has begun to explore relationships other than traditional monogamous marriages, parents worry about their children "living together"; not only our children, but we ourselves are often faced nowadays with decisions to be made about "open marriages." We won't spend a lot of time on this, but you should know that such arrangements are neither the panacea that many young people think they are, nor the devastating, bound- to- fail experiences that many parents fear they are. They each have their advantages and disadvantages.

Living together before marriage does give a couple the chance to truly explore their relationship so that they can either terminate it with less pain if it presents too many problems, or enter marriage on a more realistic basis. It also helps to keep sex from being the only reason for marriage, as it has often been in the past, with disastrous results. Many people, whether they live with each other for just a short time, a long time, or eventually change it to a legal marriage, derive great happiness from such an arrangement, and do so with utmost responsibility for each other and any children they may have; parental fears that one person, particularly the daughter, will get hurt, just prove unwarranted.

But it does not solve every problem: no matter how much easier it may be than in a long term marriage, separation is still painful when it occurs, usually for both parties. Problems within the relationship crop up just as they do in marriage, and may require counselling. And often, the arrangement does not really tell the couple how they will face marriage.

Some couples I am counselling report the same experience: while living together, sex was spontaneous, and fun. Once married, the men saw sex as their right, and women saw it as their duty; once sex became "work" instead of "play," sexual problems ensued. Whether married or not, then, your children will need sensitivity, honesty, and commitment to another human being.

A problem many parents face is what to do when their children come home for a short visit with their partner in tow. Should they let the couple share a bedroom or not? It seems to me that parents have the right to say what is acceptable behavior in their home, and that children should respect that. Rules can be set without being either nasty or insensitive. But many people find that once confusion about protocol is overcome and feelings are aired, they can accept the arrangement and almost forget the lack of a marriage license.

Open contract marriages take many forms. "Swinging," which is one of the more common, is an exchange of sexual partners by two or three couples, or a group exchange of partners at a party where anonymity is preserved and close interpersonal relationships are prevented, in order to safeguard the marital relationship. Another form of open contract is merely an agreement that each partner is free to engage in other sexual relationships.

Again, there are both advantages and disadvantages to these marriage contracts. The open marriage certainly allows for a variety that may enhance sexual activity, and abolishes the need for "infidelity." If the marriage is basically sound, both partners are completely willing, can communicate well, make the contract terms clear, and are able to reevaluate every so often and change the terms as needed, then open contracts can often enhance an already good relationship. All that sounds easier, however, than it is. Often the whole thing becomes unworkable when one member goes beyond the terms of the contract, when one partner finds it harder to deal with than anticipated, when an emotional attachment grows between one person and the extra marital partner, or when some unforeseen outside factor creates a problem. Also it can be less "open" than it looks: one partner may be using it as a guilt reliever for infidelity, with no real concern for the spouse, or it may be a last desperate and usually useless attempt to prop up a poor marriage.

Unless an abundance of honesty, empathy and concern is used, an open contract can create far more problems than it solves or prevents, and any couple thinking of using it might well consider using professional help while making the decision.

HOMOSEXUALITY

So far we've focused on heterosexual behaviors. But homosexuality is a rather common deviation from the norm in sexuality, and like masturbation, is not only of great concern to many parents and children, but is also the subject of a great deal of confusion, misinformation, and unwarranted fear. So let's spend a little more time on it.

Homosexuals are people who choose to satisfy their sexual needs with someone of their own gender. Many men in the homosexual community prefer to be called "gay," and call heterosexuals "straight"; often women prefer to be called "Lesbians." Sometimes those terms will be used here, too.

Actually, however, the definition isn't all that simple. Some people think about homosexual behavior or even have homosexual fantasies during heterosexual intercourse, yet never engage in homosexual behavior. Other people choose it only part of the time, and many teenagers engage in homosexual sex play, often to orgasm, merely as a form of masturbation or out of curiosity, and would never consider it as a way of life.

Statistics are so confusing that we can hardly tell what the incidence of homosexuality is. Kinsey reported that 37 percent of all men and 13 percent of all women had reached orgasm during homosexual behavior, and that at least 60 percent of all boys had tried it out by the age of fifteen. He also devised a seven point rating scale to show a continuum of degrees of homosexuality, with "no homosexuality" at one extreme, "exclusive homosexuality" at the other, and 50-50 in the middle. After the age of fifteen, approximately 10 per cent of the male population and a much lower percentage of the women expressed exclusive homosexual preference.   The scale shows correctly that homosexuality can exist in varying degrees.   But more recent researchers, such as Hunt, point out that it does not take into account people who may have tried it out only once in their entire lives, or people who may change the degree of preference from time to time.   When other statistical problems are taken into account, people who consider themselves exclusively homosexual is possibly a bit lower than Kinsey thought. (Hunt, 1974).

The most we can say, then, is that while gays have become more open, homosexuality does not seem to be on the rise.   It is one of the larger minorities, yet still very much a minority in terms of numbers. Differentiating between the person, the behavior, and the life style is extremely difficult.   Consequently, the labels we give people are both harmful and misleading.

Here, then, are some questions people often ask about homosexuality:

How did gays get that way?

Gays sometimes ask, "How did you get to be straight?" You probably don't know. It just happened. The causes for homosexuality are as varied as causes of anything else, and there's probably no single cause for any given individual, but rather a combination of factors. There have been many theories including hormonal imbalance, which some studies prove true, while others prove wrong. For some it may be a question of poor parental relationships, inability to live up to parental expectations, or one parent being too overbearing and the other too shadowy or weak. But you can say the same things about many other people who are not gay, and many gays come from "average" homes, having had a "good" relationship with parents who seem no different from any other parents. The fact is that we still don't really know what causes it. It is nobody's "fault," except when some kids get labeled incorrectly as "queer," then find themselves isolated, and think they have no other choice.

Are gays sick? Do they need to be cured?

Homosexuality used to be called a psychiatric illness, but that was probably because the only gays who sought psychiatrists' help went because of emotional illness. By that standard, we might also think that all straights are sick, because most people who go to psychiatrists are straight.

The American Psychiatric Association recently removed the label of "sickness" from homosexuality. More and more, professionals are beginning to think of it as either a bit of specific behavior or a general type of lifestyle that is merely different, and to assess whether it is helpful or harmful to any given individual. When people are dissatisfied with their homosexuality and wish to change it, then we try to help them do so. If they are happy with it but want to solve a particular problem in their situation, we try to help them solve that problem. If they are happy and not hurting anyone else, there is no "problem".

Can they be changed?

If a gay really wants to change, then many forms of treatment have proven helpful. Often people ask to change, however, because they have been taught that homosexuality is bad, and they are trying to conform to please others. More and more therapists are beginning to consider it more appropriate to help people accept themselves as worthwhile no matter what their sexual preference, and to help people choose on the basis of their real needs, rather than on the basis of guilt feelings.

Do they do weird things?

In activities with each other, gays have one less option than straights: they can't have intercourse with a penis in a vagina, and therefore can't make babies. Other than that, what they do is pretty similar to what other people do. They caress, use manual, oral, and sometimes anal stimulation to orgasm. Their object choice is the only difference.

Are they promiscuous?

Any minority group not allowed the options open to others will develop its own subculture that varies slightly from the major culture. Sometimes, because of discrimination that requires them to find sexual gratification furtively and quickly, many gays do "cruise," have "one night stands," and often end up with venereal disease. But then so do many straights who have no such excuse. The gay subculture does take a more casual attitude toward sex, with even people in enduring relationships using an "open contract." But then that's becoming more and more true of heterosexuals, too. As with straights, many gays, especially as our society becomes more accepting, have a warm lasting relationship with one person only, spending only a small part of their time having sex; most of the time they are teaching, driving busses, going to school, healing the sick, practicing law, fixing dinner, listening to music, lying in the sun, or doing any of the many other things people do in and out of work. Their sexuality is second in importance. First and foremost, they are people.

Can you always spot a homosexual?

The "effeminate" stereotype for men and "butch" stereotype for women is misleading. There are very "masculine" looking football players who are gay. Many men perceived as "effeminate" are totally heterosexual. There are very beautiful lesbians, and very masculine-looking straight women. Effeminacy is in the minority even in the gay community, and sometimes occurs only temporarily, just after a man has "come out" openly as gay.

During sex, does one person play the man and the other a woman?

Homosexuals don't question their identity (gender); it's merely their object choice that is different from that of a straight relationship. A man may feel proud of his masculinity, but choose a partner who is equally masculine; the same goes for a woman.

But many people are confused about this, because they see men dressing as women. Such people are called cross-dressers. Many of them are "transvestites," people (mainly, and according to many studies, perhaps only men) who receive sexual gratification from cross-dressing. Many happily heterosexually married men enjoy cross-dressing, with no desire to be women or to engage in homosexual activity. (Such cross-dressing is not be be confused with styles of dress, such as wearing caftans or pantsuits). A few of them are "transsexuals," who really do question their identity. They feel like members of the opposite sex, and sometimes undergo surgery to change their actual gender. A transsexual man, for instance, feels like a woman trapped in a male body. He may have sex with another man, and to the outside world, it looks like a homosexual relationship. But to that man, it is heterosexual, for he considers himself a woman. If he has surgery, he may be able to function as a woman in many ways, possibly even marrying and having intercourse. But many transsexuals are not so interested in sexual activity as they are in being part of the general life of the opposite gender, and have felt that way since their earliest childhood.

Do homosexuals try to seduce or rape children or adults?

Very few adults, whether gay or straight, are sexually interested in children, and very few adults, whether gay or straight, go in for rape. Most studies show that over ninety percent of reported incidents of child molestation are incurred by heterosexuals, not homosexuals. Most gays are given enough trouble as it is, without taking a chance on getting jailed or killed. With rapes you hear about in prison, it is not sex as much as violence and power that is the issue with sex merely a convenient hook on which to hang power. Also, prisoners, who have no other options for tension release than themselves or each other, are apt to turn to each other.

Will association with gays influence children or turn them gay?

Unless a child has no other options, you needn't fear "undue influence" by gays. Many homosexuals have children from a previous heterosexual marriage, and many who engage in homosexual behavior occasionally are also heterosexually married, with children. Their children can grow up to be as straight as the next person, and why not? After all, as gays point out, *their* parents were straight, and it didn't change *their* minds, so why should the converse not be equally true?

Some parents fear that a homosexual teacher or scout leader will try to influence or seduce their children. But as adults, they are not apt to be interested in children sexually, and furthermore, they can be expected to behave in accordance with the ethics of their job or profession. Interestingly enough, though, we often know that male heterosexual teachers flirt with pretty high school and college coeds and even marry them, and unless such behavior is carried to extremes, we don't think much about it.

What can I do to keep my child from being homosexual?

Try not to worry about it. You can make sure your children have members of both sexes for companionship. You can try not to make them the sons or daughters you wish you'd had, and avoid setting up unattainable goals for being a "perfect lady" or "All- American boy". This last means avoiding rigid definitions of masculinity and femininity. For example, if you panic just because a boy likes sewing or doesn't like football, call him Sissy any time he cries or expresses feelings, or if you refuse to show him tenderness just because he's male, he might associate masculinity with inhumanness. You might convince him that his human feelings are a sign that he is gay, and he may act accordingly. He may feel so unsure of himself that he will not risk heterosexual activity for fear of failure. At the other extreme, if you constantly dress him in girls' clothing, over protect him and refuse him heterosexual opportunities, he may decide to please you by not being interested in the opposite sex, or he may indeed, have no heterosexual options.

Such extremes, however, are not that common, and parents do not have control over what will happen. If your child does eventually announce that he or she is gay, you needn't feel you've failed as a parent. Your only responsibility then will be to be honest about your feelings, to be as accepting as possible, to know that he or she can be happy and responsible whether gay or straight. So think of your children as human beings, rather than potential straights or gays. Do your best to be good models for affectionate and caring husbands, wives and parents.

What if my religion says that. homosexuality is immoral?

Many churches have changed their opinions about homosexuality, and you might try talking to a few church leaders about the subject. Or you might try talking with some gay ministers, usually found in the Metropolitan Community Church. You may be able to accept their interpretation of the Bible. If you can't, that's your decision to make. Just remember that other people have the right to make their own decisions about morality. You can still respect them for their other qualities. You can still teach your children to treat all people with respect, regardless of their color, creed, politics, health, or sexual choice.

To whom can I talk to better understand homosexuality?

If there is no Metropolitan Community Church in your community, you can talk to anyone in a "Gay Liberation" group, or learn the resources from a crisis center, a mental health or social agency or even from a friend who is openly gay. The more people you talk to, the more you'll realize that there is no such thing as "The Homosexual", any more than there is "The Heterosexual", and that like all other people, gays differ widely in their personalities, biases, and even their ideas about homosexuality. You need not be embarrassed, if you are really trying to understand; most gays nowadays will understand your concerns, and try to answer your questions as well as possible. If you use some sensitivy and tact, and avoid personal, offensive questions that you would not want to be asked about your own sexual activity they will be anxious to help you understand them.

If your teenager feels that he or she is in conflict about homosexuality, you should certainly try to get him or her counselling from someone who will not try to push him or her in either direction. Such counsellors can be hard to find, but they do exist and your children should know that.

A comment of my own:

If I seem to spend a lot of time on homosexuality, it's because I am concerned about the many anonymous calls I receive from teenagers panicked about what they *think* might be homosexuality, and who are afraid to talk with their parents. Whether they are gay or not is of less concern to me than their panic. I think it a tragedy that the word *homosexual* should produce the kind of fear and self hate I hear in their voices, and that they feel so unable to turn for help to the parents they need so desperately. Not only your knowledge but your willingness to discuss such subjects can do a lot to prevent such panic. Just as important is your modeling. You can avoid using and discourage your children's use of words like fag, fairy, homo, or queer and the joking about or taunting of people who dress or act "differently". Such words are at the top of my dirty word list, along with sick, abnormal, frigid, impotent, stupid, retard, nigger and honky. I consider them far worse than some of the four letter sexual words, because they're cruel, unfair putdowns that assault human dignity. That's *my* opinion, of course. More important is the need for you to think about *yours*.

CHAPTER ELEVEN

SEX EDUCATION IN THE SCHOOLS

For teachers and counsellors, and for parents
whose children are taught by them

In talking with teachers I find that there are three things that worry them most about sex education.

1. They feel they don't know enough, might give wrong information, not know an answer, and either hurt a child or look foolish.

2. They fear that if they mention sex, some parent will complain to the principal (unless they are the principal, which is even worse), try to get them fired, and have their names plastered across the headlines as corrupters of innocent children.

3. They don't know how to start.

Let's take the easiest problem first: starting.

Often people fear starting because they're thinking mainly about formal courses, or about biology, which may sound frightening to a kindergarten or English teacher. Formal courses are not the only way to give planned sex education in schools: in fact, they're not really the best way. They're much stiffer, they catch students at the point of the school's interest instead of the children's interest and there's a tendency to stick to a curriculum that does not fit the children's needs at that time.

The easiest way to start, then, is to keep your eyes and ears open for good door openers. The earlier you start, the easier it is.

Little children, still thinking about people as people, rather than as boys and girls, are not so embarrassed—though they might be giggly and silly at first. If they get used to the terms and to talking about sex early, when the subject is simpler, you've got a head start for later, when they're more embarrassed and the subject is more complicated. Here are some common examples of door openers.

In nursery school or kindergarten, while the children were going to the bathroom, the teacher asked casually, "How many know why the boys go to the toilet standing up, and the girls sit down?"

A child announced in Show and Tell that he had a new baby sister. Instead of merely saying "that's nice," the teacher began talking about babies, and at art time, had the children draw how they thought babies looked inside their mothers. That led into a discussion of how children really feel about new arrivals in the family.

A fourth grader yelled "fuck" on the playground, and got a lot of shocked attention. The playground teacher calmly gathered the kids around. They began talking about why such words upset adults, and questions about sex came pouring out naturally.

A teacher heard some teenagers teasing someone about being *queer*. She mentioned in class that she thought people had a lot of questions about homosexuality. This led to a discussion not only about that subject, but about general ideas on masculinity and femininity, and attitudes toward difference. Later, a member of the gay community spoke to the class and a lot of stereotypes were broken down. No, nobody converted, but the teasing of certain children stopped, and the original victim learned that he was not, after all, "queer."

A group of older children were seen showing each other pornography. Instead of confiscating the material, the teacher joined the group; together they looked at the pictures and discussed the ways in which they were realistic or unrealistic and the attitudes implied. Again questions began pouring out, and instead of misinformation, the children got correct answers and more responsible values.

One of the best examples of serendipity I've seen once came from my daughter's teacher; when I later analyzed what had happened, it showed the kind of interplay and reinforcement that can take place between home, school, and child, when both teacher and parents are using serendipity.

My daughter had asked for help with an oral report each student was to give on "growing up in primitive tribes." I suddenly remembered that when we had gone to Africa a few years earlier, we had visited a certain tribe, seen a ritual circumcision dance which she had been too young to understand, and had brought home a book about that tribe that she had never been willing to read. I brought out the book, reminded her of the dance we had seen and not only was she willing to read it, but the memories she had took on new meaning. She came home from school glowing; her teacher and class had been fascinated and she had received an "A." That was my use of serendipity for general education. But her teacher took it one step farther by asking the students if they knew what circumcision means, and the ensuing discussion led to further discussion of how sex is viewed in different cultures. Her casual attitude did more than give facts: it helped reinforce my attitude that sex is a discussable subject, enhancing communication between me and my daughter, and easing communication between her and her friends.

So even though we hadn't gone to Africa in order to help her in this class, and even though her teacher had not planned the assignment to give sex education, our mutual use of serendipity helped each other and provided door openers for the entire class. This teacher was doing what I can only assume was some beautiful planned sex education.

Formal course starters:

Formal courses do have their place. They may be the only way to open the door, or the best way to pull together bits and pieces of information into a cohesive body of knowledge, weeding out misinformation. Even they can start with door openers based on where students are at any given moment.

One might start with a discussion on censorship or on some controversial movie. One might note the fact that the biology book or the health book had left out sex, and have the class discuss why that might have happened. One might start a discussion on why people are so hesitant to talk about sex, or about the common problems that the particular age group faces. Or one might have the children write unsigned questions, and choose the starter according to what seems to be the main interest.

Tip:

"Looseners" are good starters which ease communication, especially for teenagers who may be embarrassed.

I once had a class of fourteen year olds so embarrassed we couldn't even mention the word "baby" without someone starting to giggle and snicker. So we spent the first session just calling out and writing on the blackboard every word we could think of about sex, dirty and otherwise. For a while the place sounded like a zoo, as people (myself included) released their tension with laughter. We finally reached the point where we could get through a sentence and then a question without someone dying of embarrassment. Only then could we hold meaningful discussions.

Tip:

Humor eases a lot of tension. It's also a lot of fun!

HOW MUCH DOES A TEACHER NEED TO KNOW?

Teachers are responsible for knowing enough facts both about biology and general sexual behavior to give reasonably correct information. Even more important is the ability to discern between fact and opinion, to admit the lack of knowledge and to either call in the expert who has that knowledge or to help the children use another resource. Equally important is the ability to legitimize differences of opinion, and to encourage the children to discuss things with their own parents.

They should know at least the facts given in Chapter 10, and possibly more facts about birth control and venereal disease. I would urge teachers—especially those conducting formal sex education classes—to augment those facts through further reading, classes, or workshops. Courses may be offered by local universities, community social agencies, sex therapists, or sex educators. Such courses or workshops do far more than provide additional information, for participants usually cite the exchange of ideas, the viewing of films, and the thinking through of values and teaching techniques as the most valuable parts of the program.

The "Don't-Should" and the "Plumbing" approaches to sex education.

Many teachers seem to feel that they need to know all about biology and hygiene, and that that is all they need to teach. This is often called the "Plumbing" approach. Or they give a few moral platitudes, like "Don't have intercourse before you're married," "Do remember to keep your legs crossed," "Don't cheapen sex." Thus they think they've instilled values. Many school programs give a few facts about menstruation, reproduction, some facts about hygiene, and may show some diagrams and cross sections, mostly of fallopian tubes, ovaries, and penises. But that sort of biology is probably the least important part of sex education.

I know of one sex educator who gets so angry at the "Plumbing" approach that he has been known to get up in front of a group of teachers in a workshop, wave his arms around and yell, "Fallopian tubes, fallopian tubes—who cares about fallopian tubes? Damn the fallopian tubes!" And cross sections of penises don't tell anybody anything. In fact, some filmstrips I have seen in school programs give misinformation. The narrator is talking about reproduction, which can only take place with an erect penis, while the pictures show a non-erect one. Such courses can be totally boring and almost useless. It's no wonder that students turn to pornography—they figure they'll get more information. And too often they're right!

What do children want to know?

Some biology, of course, is both interesting and necessary. But the point of that biology is how it will affect kids and what to do about it, and *that's* what's usually left out.

My daughter saw the same film on menstruation in the fourth, fifth, and sixth grade, and that was the extent of her formal school sex education. My son had a better program in his school, and quickly learned more technical and biological definitions than I know. But when I asked if the teacher ever talked about things that we had discussed, like responsibility for one's behavior, the effects of masturbation, petting, or the problems and pleasures of sexuality, he looked amazed and said, "Gosh, no! Was he supposed to? Is that what sex education means?"

What young people really want to know is what's happening with and how to react to their bodies and how they compare with other people, what thoughts and behaviors are acceptable, and how babies are made and what the future holds. No one age has a priority on these interests. As in teaching all subjects, so in sex, we give small amounts of information in the early grades, gradually adding both in scope and depth each year.

Little children will then be more interested in babies and how they come to be, a bit interested in adult behavior, and very interested in how they themselves should behave. Older children will need more detail on reproduction, their own behavior including masturbation, and how their bodies will soon begin to change. The teenagers will want a lot of detail on a wide range of subjects, with emphasis on masturbation, intercourse, reproduction, childbirth, and birth control.

Teenagers are particularly concerned about the physical and emotional changes they are undergoing, and how they should handle themselves. They worry about how masculine or feminine they are, how attractive and normal they are, how to cope with the opposite sex, and what values they should have. The hygiene and biology they need is only helpful if it relates to those concerns.

Sometimes adult insensitivity to adolescent worries leads to seemingly unrelated problems. While I was a supervisor in a juvenile office one year, one of my workers was asked to work with a fifteen year old delinquent referred by the school because of truancy, disobedience, and "sassing" the teacher. Only because of a hunch based on some chance remark reported by the social worker, did I think to explore sex as an underlying factor. It turned out that all three offenses were directly related to acute embarrassment about undressing in front of other boys, hence his refusal to attend gym or swimming class, shower, or to wear gym shorts. Had the parents or teacher been more able to talk with him about sex, had the school offered sex education either in classes or via the school counsellor, to enable adolescents to discuss adolescent worries, had there been made some provision for privacy in locker rooms —any one of these might have prevented the entire problem.

Insensitivity did not stop there, however. The boy was to be admitted back to school only if he submitted to a formal paddling by the principal, who was convinced that the presence of witnesses would safeguard the student's rights, and that the boy would then thank him for his lesson in "how to take punishment like a man." Reluctantly I agreed to let the social worker act as one of the witnesses, on the grounds that at least the boy knew him to be a sympathetic supporter.

I was wrong! I would never again allow anyone under my supervision to participate in such an act—and would assist the parents in seeking legal help to fight such a punishment. The boy was not grateful, did not see his witnesses as supporters, but rather felt that he had been let down by his parents, social worker, school, and society in general. I am forced to agree with his assessment. He felt so humiliated that he ran away the next day, and never returned to school.

The only benefit gained from that experience was that once alerted to such feelings, both the teacher and I became more sensitive and were able to prevent such tragedies in the future. I don't know how many similar events take place elsewhere, but I am convinced that if we, as parents, teachers, social workers, and citizens were more sensitive both in our ways of preventing problems and in solving them, we could be far more helpful to our young people.

What do children need to know?

They need to know what they want to know. Teenagers also need to know about possible consequences of sexual behavior, and how to protect themselves against such undesirable consequences as unwanted babies and venereal disease. Some teachers avoid these subjects at all cost, while others focus solely on the terrible things that can happen to a sexually active adolescent. The first approach avoids facts necessary for developing responsible sexual behavior. The second approach really teaches—in an unplanned way—that sex is dirty and evil. While it may frighten children, it won't stop them from being sexually active, and it won't help them be responsible.

Are teachers responsible for giving values and opinions?

When it comes to values and opinions, it's the same to me whether the subject is sex, politics, or religion. I feel that not only do they have their place, but they're very important, *provided that they're clearly differentiated from facts.* I don't mind if my child's teacher disagrees with me in politics; I don't even care if I think he or she has gotten a few facts wrong, if they're not particularly harmful. But I expect that my child will not be given harmful information, and I expect allowance to be made for different interpretations even of some facts.

It's the same for sex. If a teacher errs on some obscure biological process that makes no difference to anyone but a doctor, I don't care much. I think all teachers should know whether or not masturbation is harmful; but if one admits to not knowing and promises to find out or to provide an expert who does know, I consider that a sensible and valid approach. If a teacher says that his or her religion approves or disapproves of masturbation, but that many people are of a different opinion and the teacher advises students to talk with their own parents about it, I consider that a valid approach. But if a teacher says that masturbation is immoral, that's an unfair imposition of a personal value. If he or she says that masturbation is harmful, that's absolutely incorrect information. Moreover, while it won't stop children from masturbating, it may frighten them, and may have serious emotional consequences. I consider both statements very harmful, and I'll object. This, of course, brings us to the worry that's hardest to deal with:

HOW ARE PARENTS GOING TO REACT?

It's probably the fear of incurring parental wrath that makes teachers stick so firmly to "plumbing." Biology may require some review but it's safer; you run less risk of conflicting with parents' views.

The teachers' fears, however, are usually unwarranted. Parents who object to sex education in the schools do so either because they are afraid their children will be told "anything goes," they are afraid the children will be told sex is dirty and evil, or that no matter what the kids are told, they as parents will lose importance. Once they find that none of these things happen, they usually relax.

Often teachers report that if there is any problem at all, it is the exact opposite of complaints about content. Instead, some parents relax so much that they absolutely refuse to get involved, and force the school to become totally responsible for their children's planned sex education.

Whether parents complain or not, however, I firmly believe that parents and teachers have a real responsibility to each other for the sake of the child, and that any sex education program is only as good as the parents' involvement. I strongly suspect that the major reason for parental objections is that the schools have not involved parents in the process, that parents don't know what's happening, and are concerned, *as they should be*. Only if the program fills in gaps and opens three-way doors between parents, teachers, and children, can a program be a real success.

Opening three-way doors:

There are many ways to do this, depending on the size of the school and the amount of time and personnel available. Here is an ideal way. Suppose you're starting a formal program. After your own basic planning, you might send a letter to all parents, sharing your tentative curriculum, including the values you plan to stress, asking for their input. You might hold both a planning meeting and periodic planned sessions to discuss particular topics, to let parents know what you are doing, and to plan how you will handle differences in values. You might also let them read, view, and help select the materials to be used; you'll be surprised how helpful they can be.

Of course if two parents who raised no fuss at all until they saw your outline then misinterpret it or get upset by it, you'll wish you'd left well enough alone. Sometimes the group can change their minds when you alone can't. If they're right, you'd better be finding it out early and giving your plan more thought. If they're wrong, better to find it out quickly with the group behind you, than to have them storming in six months later, complaining they had no idea what was going on, and threatening to go to the state legislature. Chances are, your biggest worry will be that no one shows up for anything, not even a routine parent-child conference. With a record of your invitations, if uninvolved parents have gripes, they'll have only themselves to blame, and you'll be protected.

Suppose you get into an informal discussion, or that someone gets upset or misinterprets during a class? We all know that students can go home and tell parents, "I can have intercourse before I'm married. Teacher said so!" or "Why can't I say "fuck?" Teacher lets me." Children can say you told dirty stories in class and forced them to read dirty books. They can hear you all wrong, get the facts garbled, and leave you sounding like a terrible teacher. They can take you up on your suggestion that they talk to their parents, and the parents, caught by surprise, can call you up in a furor because they felt like fools.

Such problems can be handled by anticipating and dealing with them before they occur. You might send occasional reminders that their feedback is important. You might send notes home that venereal disease, for example, was discussed today, and that if parents have questions or wish to know what was said, they should feel free to contact you. If a particular problem occurs, you may wish to send a personal note or make a phone call to a particular parent. Or you might merely include discussion of the program during your usual parent-teacher conferences.

When I started a sex education program for retarded children in a school of a different faith than my own, everyone, including myself was apprehensive. We did have some minor disagreements and parental concerns, of course, but the only "problem" in two years turned out to be related to an entirely different matter. Even parents who were viewed by the staff as habitual complainers were pleased, stating that it was the first time they'd felt so involved with the school, or that their opinions had been both sought and respected. The only complaint was that more parents didn't get involved. When children did misinterpret or get upset—and they often did in such a school—parents called to let me know and to find out what had happened. We planned strategy together and operated as teams. That didn't mean that things always ran smoothly or that there weren't mistakes made. Textbooks go along like clockwork; life seldom does.

My experience was in a small school where I was allowed considerable flexibility and freedom, and where contact with parents was easy and direct. I can understand why sometimes my suggestions draw strong protests from teachers in a large public school system. Their curriculums are set and standardized, and they are struggling just to obtain reasonably sized classrooms, preparation time and truly free time away from school, without taking on extra tasks in and out of school hours.

It doesn't take much time or paperwork, however, to prepare standarized forms to be used when messages to parents are necessary, and involving parents does not mean checking with them every time a new idea is introduced. Nor need it mean that parents will start interfering, as many teachers fear they will. It only means that párental concerns are recognized and their rights are protected.

Audio-visual aids are useful. So are texts with humor, explicit pictures, anatomical models from medical supply houses or universities, and humorous stories. Too many teachers, afraid they'll be accused of showing pornography or telling dirty jokes, make the most interesting subject in the world the most boring, thereby giving unplanned messages that contradict the messages they are trying to give.

It's often helpful to have one staff person act as coordinator, planner, and trouble shooter, with final responsibility. This is true even if sex education is a total school program in which each teacher provides his or her own ideas. Only one person then has to answer questions or face upset parents. He or she may offer assistance to both parents and teachers and provide continuity to the program, seeing that there is some consistency in stressed values, despite minor differences among teachers. If parents know that there's one person who can be counted on for help, they may feel considerably reassured. The staff coordinator can be a teacher knowledgeable in the area of sex, a social worker, psychologist, or school counsellor —whoever has the most expertise.

Make use of consultants and guest lecturers.

Guest lecturers break up the monotony. One human being talking informally about his or her lifestyle, problems or concerns can act as a clincher to reinforce what you or your textbook say, or may act as a door opener for problems difficult for you to introduce on your own.

There are experts in most cities today who can speak to the class or help you with the program. Social workers and psychologists may be most helpful, but it will depend on your particular community. Doctors are usually everybody's favorite, and can be counted on for help in "plumbing" (biology). A good part of sexuality, however, has little to do with medicine, and a medical degree does not ensure knowledge about sexuality. Psychiatrists, ministers, and educators may also be helpful and Planned Parenthood Clinics are always willing to provide advisors and lecturers.

Remember that while sex has been around for a long time, sexuality as a field of study has not. Few experts today, even in medical school, unless they are just out of school or have gone back for continued education, have probably had formal courses in sexuality. Those who teach formal courses have come from a variety of fields: for example, psychology, sociology, social work, medicine, education, and biology. I have mentioned social workers several times. This does not mean I consider others less knowledgeable—I simply know more about my own profession. Too, people used to thinking of social workers as welfare workers, may not realize that trained social workers should have basic competence, and may have specialized training in such areas as sex counselling and education, marital counselling, and psychotherapy.

People who have little knowledge at all other than about their own behavior, pass themselves off as experts. Within a few years there should be a good core of people with special training, but right now their numbers are relatively few. So know your individual and his or her qualifications!

Don't overlook the experts in your midst

Too many teachers feel that only those from outside their school are experts. Your own school social worker, counsellor, or psychologist may be the most knowledgeable person in the community, or may know the appropriate resources for help. In-school consultants can be especially helpful. They can help plan, teach, assist you in formulating your own ideas, help you out of a hole, help you with an irate parent or an irate colleague. They can also help in interpreting the program or working with a parent who has special concerns. Remember that the key word here is *help,* not *find fault.* How can they criticize? They don't know all the answers anymore than you do, no matter what their expertise. They will only pool their knowledge with yours, and together you can struggle through in a common cause.

Make use of educational facilities for yourself:

There are often workshops or classes in the community to help you gain knowledge and to think through your ideas about sex. It will be worth your effort to attend. If you can't, some other staff member or consultant may have done so and will be able to share information with you.

Keep the program flexible and use creativity:

Just because you start with one plan doesn't mean you have to stay with it. In fact, breaking things up once in a while will provide new ideas and avoid monotony. You may have planned a course for eight weeks; but if one class only needs two or three weeks, why continue? Most children find it difficult to talk with parents around, but if you sense that a "rap" session between parents and kids might be helpful, why not take a chance? As you will see, I stress keeping the boys and girls together. There are times, however, when girls may need to talk with girls alone and boys with boys alone. Certainly flexibility and creativity are more difficult in a large system, but in my experience, that has never seemed to stop good teachers in any subject, and that is probably what makes them good teachers.

Team teaching is especially useful in sex education:

Team teaching allows one person to observe while the other does the teaching; it enables each teacher to be helped out of any holes, gives two viewpoints, and where there is disagreement, provides a model for respecting other opinions. If the team has one male and one female, it provides the viewpoint of each sex, and more easily allows for small group discussion at any point where separation of sexes might be useful.

Don't forget the commonplace:

Sometimes we get so focused on the intricacies of biology and physical acts, that we forget the obvious simple things of life. Young teenagers may know many facts about sexuality, yet get nervous when it comes to holding a simple conversation with a member of the opposite sex. Role playing and communication exercises, sometimes with you modeling, may be the most helpful thing you do throughout the entire course.

Take it easy:

Little bits of information every semester or year, as needed, starting with nursery school or kindergarten and continuing throughout school are better than one crash course at some magic age. By the time some schools reach their magic age, many of their students have been sexually active for years, and some are already parents. Also, if you've paved the way, even the crash courses will be easier.

Assume less knowledge rather than more:

You will need to be creative to teach basic facts without boring students who already know them, but never assume that children remember all they've been taught. Asking "Who knows? . . ." (instead of "Who doesn't know? . . . ") lets you gauge whether you need merely a refresher statement for some wavery hands, or a full scale review. A question box for anonymous questions is always useful, or a periodic request for written questions, in which everybody must hand in a paper with a question or comment, so that nobody will feel ashamed to be seen writing.

Lay ground rules and let the parents know what they are: Some of mine are:

> While humor is fine, no one can laugh at or put down another person.

> Words acceptable in class may not be acceptable elsewhere, and the class is not to be used as an excuse to shock parents.

> My opinions do not constitute permission for students to engage in any kind of sexual behavior. Students should be discussing moral questions with their parents. Parents and I can disagree without either of us being right or wrong, and parents are the final authority for children.

> I will be discussing generalities with parents, but confidences will be kept and names will not be used. If there ever is something specific I think should be discussed with a parent, I will not do so without first talking it over with the child.

In the last ground rule, I stress confidentiality because otherwise, children may be afraid to speak up. But I leave myself an out because without one, it's possible to get caught in a double bind in the unlikely event that there ever is anything I really need to tell a parent. So far that's never happened in a school situation, but even one such event could become an ethical or personal disaster.

If a problem arises, let your Principal know as quickly as possible.

Your superior will probably want to offer you all the help and support possible, even if you were at fault, but will need time. Administrators don't want to appear foolish before parents any more than teachers do. No matter what the situation, they need time to plan how to meet the needs of both parent and teacher wisely and fairly.

ISSUES TEACHERS OFTEN RAISE

Should the sexes be segregated in sex education classes?

Allowing for flexibility as the need arises, my answer is usually an emphatic "No!" Presumably your planned message is that people should be able to discuss sexual matters openly and without embarrassment. Segregation gives an unplanned message that is contradictory, for it tells students that there are some things boys and girls must not talk about together. Isn't it important for boys to know about menstruation and how girls feel about it? Isn't it important for girls to know how boys feel about changes during puberty? The fourteen year old girl who complained that boys had all the fun was dumbfounded to learn that boys get just as concerned about nocturnal emissions and erections they cannot control as girls get about menstrual accidents. She had never stopped to think how frightening it might be to do the "asking," to take a chance on being turned down or even ridiculed. She had also never considered the possibility that girls might also take responsibility for expressing interest.

Should the school or teacher get parental permission before discussing sexual matters?

Again, I usually give a definite "No" to this question. Do you ask permission to teach English? Biology? Social Science (which in itself sometimes gets into sensitive subjects)? Of course not! Why should sex be any different?

When teachers ask permission, they are doing two unplanned things: 1. They're telling both students and parents that sex education is a dangerous area that may be hazardous to the health. In other words, they're issuing a warning. I don't think that is the intended message. 2. They're not really saying what they intend to do or plan to teach. If I were a parent concerned that my child was going to be corrupted, I'd certainly feel I was signing a blank check, and would refuse permission. If I were concerned that my child would be told sex was dirty and evil, I'd feel that I was signing a blank check with a hint of what might get filled in the spaces. I'd be tempted to refuse, would give permission only to avoid being misinterpreted, and then would resent feeling trapped.

What parents want and need much more than being asked permission, is recognition of their right to know that their children will be taught by knowledgeable, responsible people, who will respect and impart parental values, and who will include them in the process. Telling them what you are planning to teach and asking for their ideas is far better than asking for permission. It gives them information they need to make wise decisions, demonstrates that you are responsible and concerned, and are not asking them to sign blank checks. You will probably get few or no complaints, some people asking valid questions and many people saying "Great! It's about time!"

Sometimes these flowery predictions just don't come true. It seems to be a truism that the kids who most need help from the school are the only ones whose parents refuse to let them get it, no matter how well you handle things. What can be done? Head for your nearest social worker or counsellor and ask for help. This is his or her area of expertise. If your expert does no better or feels that it would make matters worse to intervene, you'll have to make your peace with the problem. Even aside from legal factors in parental versus school rights, you do not want to get children caught in a decision of whether to believe you or their parents. That sort of conflict can do more damage than anything else. Even under such adverse conditions, it will often be possible for you and your consultant to work out some other way of helping such children—either individually or perhaps indirectly through a general classroom discussion on parent-child relationships.

What about birth control and venereal disease questions?

I myself feel that it is never too soon to start talking about birth control. Little children need no more than the knowledge that sometimes people decide not to have babies and take steps to prevent having them. The age at which more detail is needed will depend on the children and the milieu in which they live. Early adolescents should know the basics about contraceptives and where they can go for help as well as something about venereal disease prevention and cure. High school students should know as much detail as possible. This does not give permission and should be so stated; but withholding information does not discourage activity, it merely increases chances of problems. Many premarital pregnancies and venereal diseases could be prevented if teenagers were told the problems with "withdrawal," the usefullness of con-

......, and the fact that there are alternatives to intercourse in sexual expression.

But as noted earlier, facts are not enough, and values may actually be easier to instill in a classroom discussion with peers, than they are in private talks with parents. Giving information and values tends to promote responsibility, not discourage it. This is true even if some students' religion forbids certain forms of birth control. No religion forbids responsible behavior!

Tip:

This is an area where medical personnel will be helpful, and where parents will certainly want to know that values are being taught.

Tip:

I am sometimes asked how to maintain integrity and still respect conflicting parental values, when dealing with a particular child about some concern such as masturbation. In such a situation, I might remind children that parents are trying to do what they feel is best, and that children should try to respect their parents' wishes. But I add that if they find this impossible at times, they needn't feel they are terrible people—*many children* have the same problem; adults often disagree about such issues, and they will decide for themselves, when they are older, what *they* believe. This addition does not undermine parents, but maintains integrity and relieves undue guilt on the part of the child. There will also be times when parents may want to use similar techniques for maintaining their rights without undermining the teacher.

AN ASIDE TO PARENTS

Courses in school make great door openers for you. But you need to know what is happening. Don't assume that all is great, ask!

My husband and I were afraid that our son, who had a lot of information from us, would be bored by his school program. One day we asked how he liked it. "Great!" he said, "I'm learning a lot I didn't know." We were a bit miffed, *though we shouldn't have been,* to think that the son of two sex educators should have to learn things from a gym teacher. (By the way, I've frequently wondered why gym teachers are so often assigned sex education classes. I suspect sometimes those gym teachers wonder, too). At any rate, we asked what he had learned. "I learned about masturbation," he said. We had talked about that with him, but he evidently hadn't understood and we were pleased that the teacher had gotten the information across, even if we hadn't. Suddenly I thought to ask what he had learned. Sure enough, he still had it confused with nocturnal emissions and we had to explain again.

I'm sure we gave him correct information and I'm sure his teacher did too. But if we hadn't checked, he might still be confused. Gaps are nothing for either parent or teacher to be ashamed of. No one adult can provide all the information needed and no child can remember all the adult has provided. It is to fill in inevitable gaps and misinterpretations that schools and home combine efforts.

What if you're in doubt about a particular program?

It's often difficult for a parent to evaluate a program even when it is presented openly and honestly. It's even more difficult if all one gets is bits and pieces. Recently a friend said to me, "I'm really upset. Sally's teacher was blowing up rubbers and encouraging intercourse and telling the kids not to tell their parents what he had said." My advice in such a situation would be to refrain from panic. *Walk, don't run* to the telephone, make an appointment with the teacher or principal and discuss your concerns calmly. Often a child misinterprets or even deliberately overstates in order to shock parents. Many children sound upset as their way of trying a door opener with protection for themselves, so that you won't get angry at them, even if you're upset about the class discussion.

A few days later that same friend and I were talking to a third parent, who told us about the wonderful program her daughter was in. Her child had come home talking about the information she had received about rubbers and asking a lot of questions. It sounded as if the teacher had been creative and helpful. He had told the children to talk with their parents and this mother was delighted with the opportunity he had provided for her to discuss the topic that had been difficult for her to approach with her daughter. When the two parents compared notes, they found that their children were in the same class.

If you go storming to the teacher, you'll meet defensiveness and anger. If you are really trying to understand what has happened, any responsible educator should gladly review with you what is going on, work with you, and will be as concerned as you are if misinterpretations or teaching errors are occurring. You need not be concerned about disagreements in values, as long as you can work out a way of handling them so that neither you nor the teacher will be undermined. Eventually the child will decide for him or her self what he or she thinks. The more calm and rational your approach, the more impact you will have on that decision.

If you feel your concerns are disregarded, that the child is getting harmful information and the program is poor, then certainly you should take your concerns to a higher authority. However, you might want to discuss them with some reputable community expert before doing so.

At any rate, fight the *right* fight. Don't waste time fighting *against* sex education in the schools, for your child will get it even if every planned program is wiped out. Rather, fight for planned sex education that will keep you informed, reinforce your own values, and give you input when values are given with which you disagree.

Making the most of sex education:

Sex education in the schools has distinct advantages for both parents and teachers in that it can back the position you hold and reinforce your views on sexuality. At various stages, parents or teachers are held in low esteem by students. Sometimes parents are always right and teachers are always wrong, sometimes parents are the lowest on the totem pole. Peers are never lowest! Adults stand a greater chance of influencing students and offspring if they are backing each other. While peer pressure will always be a great influence on young people, school programs can both temper the bad influence and alter the peer pressure so that it becomes a welcome force instead of one to be dreaded.

General learning skills can be taught under the guise of sex education. One year, in the school for the retarded where I worked, the students became upset because I was taking too much time for planning, and the sex education course was not starting soon enough to suit them. At the same time, I was part of a committee working to establish better sex education for the retarded in the community. The students were told to petition me for an earlier starting date and were asked to help me convince people from the community that more sex education should be given to the retarded. In the process of writing a petition, discussing what they should say, getting it down on paper, preparing and orally presenting their paper to community leaders, they got practice in reading, writing, speaking, and thinking without ever thinking of it as school work. Their attention span was far greater than usual, and while they thought their English teacher was giving them time away from English grammar to work on sex education, their teacher knew she was using this to teach them English.

CHAPTER TWELVE

"PEANUTS IN THE CHINA—"

MENTAL RETARDATION* AND OTHER HANDICAPS

In general the mentally retarded have the same sexual needs and desires as any other people, the same capabilities for learning responsible behaviors as other people and the same need for sex education as others do. Many people find this hard to believe.

I was once in a workshop on sex education for the mentally retarded, in which a leading community doctor said, "I can't quite understand all this talk about sex education. You can't educate the retarded—all you can do is see they don't infest the country with retarded babies. Whenever I see a retarded girl in my office, the first thing I do is sterilize her, and then I don't give a damn what she does!"

Perhaps he thought he was being helpful, but if I had been the parent of such a patient, I would have sued him for malpractice. Still, many people, including parents of retarded children, feel the same way because of the many myths that have developed about people with intellectual disabilities. Like other myths, they can be completely contradictory and yet held simultaneously; and like other myths, they must be cleared away in order to make room for more realistic thinking. Some of them are:

---

*I use this term with misgivings, recognizing the negative and offensive impact it has come to have. The fact that there is no simple and acceptable plural adds to the problem. Yet I can find no substitute that is both suitable and simple. A more recent term, "developmentally disabled," is not only unwieldy, but in my personal opinion, is meaningless.

MYTHS ABOUT RETARDED CHILDREN

Myth—The mentally retarded are all alike.

They're not! They come in a variety of shapes, sizes, needs, and abilities just like the rest of the population. First of all, there are different degrees of impairment, falling into extremely broad categories such as "mild," "moderate," "severe," or "profound," or "educable" versus "trainable." Even such categories tell us little about individuals. Second, many people labelled "retarded" actually have "learning disabilities." While intelligent, they may be blocked in their learning and functioning at a retarded level because of emotional, social, audio, visual, or some other problem. Whatever the reason, it interferes with learning, and such children present some of the same problems in teaching that the retarded do, no matter how intelligent they are.

Some are only slightly retarded. They function pretty well on their own with minimal help from anyone and are almost indistinguishable from the rest of the community. Others will need considerable help in order to function outside an institution, and others will need a half-way house. A few will need to be institutionalized.

Even within an institution there will be differences. Most people will be able to care for themselves with some help. They will have sexual needs and desires, and will need to learn responsible and acceptable outlets for their needs. A small percentage will need the most basic care and feeding, may never have any desire or ability, sexually, to do more than stimulate themselves, and may never learn or have to be taught how to satisfy their needs in that way.

When it comes to marriage and child care, again it is highly individual. Some can marry, need little if any help, and find real joy in the close relationship. Others will need help in planning, finances, and working out interpersonal relationships. Still others will find the close relationship of a marriage too stressful to handle. Probably most will find children too much of an intellectual, financial and emotional burden, but perhaps at least a small percentage will take good care of a child with minimal help.

Some retarded persons should not have children because their retardation is inherited, while others whose handicap is due to an injury or illness, will produce beautiful, healthy, intelligent babies.

Some will be able to manage their own birth control program with little or no help, others will need a responsible person to take over the management, others will participate voluntarily in a decision to become sterilized, and still others will be unable to take part in such a decision, and will need it made for them.

Some people are visibly retarded, yet actually have only mild impairment, while others, who look normal, are actually grossly intellectually deficient.

So you see that it's almost impossible to make a generalization that will fit every retarded person's needs and abilities. All we can really be sure of is that they have the same basic needs and rights as other people, and that what differences there are from the more average citizen need not create the kind of societal panic that has led us to try to deprive them of their sexuality.

Because of these myths, we have developed a basic myth regarding sex education that seems to linger even though we have begun to dispel it for general education. That myth is:

Myth—The retarded cannot learn. Not only do they not need sex education, but providing it is an impossible task.

We are, however, becoming more and more aware that the retarded both need and are capable of using sex education. I once had a group of highly embarrassed retarded teenagers, with the same "hangups" their more intelligent counterparts had. As an opener we discussed the causes of embarrassment; as a game, I started a sentence with what their parents had told them. The sentence was "Babies come from. . ." We had all sorts of interesting answers: "Babies come from ask your mother." "Babies come from don't bother me, I'm busy." "Babies come from don't talk dirty." But one girl answered, "Babies come from the mother's uterus. And I know how, too. They come out through the vagina, and what makes them is that the man puts his penis in the woman's vagina. But you shouldn't have babies unless you can take care of them. I don't know if I want babies or not—they sound like a lot of work. But what I really wanna know is does it hurt when the man puts it in? And how old should you be?" That girl was neither older nor smarter than most of the others in her class, but she had obviously received a lot more information from her parents. Of course she was able to put things together a lot better than more severely impaired students.

Myth—The retarded remain children from birth to death and are innocent creatures who have no interest whatsoever in sex.

Yet we know now that despite individual differences, generally the bodies of these children, like others, grow to maturity, become capable of producing children, and of giving and receiving sensual pleasure. Warren Johnson, a noted sex educator, points out that the retarded share many things in common with the general population, including an interest in closeness, physical contact, affection in varying degrees, and an interest in sex, particularly in the need for sensual gratification. Winifred Kempton, known for her work with the retarded, notes that while many parents think their children are uninterested in sex, this is often because those children have sensed adult fear, repress their interest, and may lack verbal skills to make their needs known.

Myth—Adolescent, retarded males may become sex maniacs who will rape and produce more sex maniacs.

Kempton notes that there is no research to show the retarded are any more dangerous sexually than the general public. The personnel who work with them suggest that for the most part, they are gentle, anxious to please, and have suffered from lack of social skills due to little or no training, rather than being ruled by unrestrainable sex urges. Of course some people are also emotionally disturbed, but that's also true of the general population.

Myth—Retarded people have no sexual inhibitions.

There are many reasons for the seemingly uninhibited sexual behavior of many retarded teenagers and adults. We will talk more about them later, but briefly, they have more to do with lack of training and lack of private facilities than they do with lack of inhibitions. As Dr. Johnson points out, one of the things the retarded have in common with other people is their sense of guilt about sex.

Myth—The retarded are incapable of loving, marrying, caring for children, or learning responsibility.

Actually, one of the difficulties in dealing with the retarded is that they are often so very loving and anxious to please others. Many of them are quite capable of marrying, caring for children, and taking responsibility. Of course this will vary with the individual, just as it does with other people.

Myth—The retarded are like anyone else, and sex education can be exactly the same for everyone.

As a result of this myth, I have seen schools with good sex education programs fail miserably with the retarded. I once heard a psychologist tell a distraught mother that she should talk with her retarded teenage daughter about sex just the way she would with any of her other children—that there was no difference. Essentially he was right, and he meant to reassure her. But he merely made her feel more helpless, because she knew perfectly well that there were differences, and that she could not treat all her children the same way.

There are problems facing anyone who tries to help retarded children or adults regarding sex. Ignoring them does not make them go away. Those problems do not *decrease* the need for planned sex education—they *increase* it. Nor do they mean a hopeless monumental task, if one recognizes what the difficulty really is. In my experience, that difficulty seems to be mainly that any problem that is true in education for the average child is even more true with the retarded person. Anything you do for the average person you must do even more for the retarded person.

REALITIES

How does that translate? It means that if all children need basic simple concepts and vocabulary as early as possible, retarded children need them even more. If all children need door openers to stimulate thinking and discussion, retarded children need them more. If all children are "concrete" (i.e., they learn through seeing, feeling, touching—any way that helps them understand processes that they cannot actually see), retarded children are more so and need more "concrete" techniques than other children do. If all children need a certain amount of repetition, retarded children need even more. If all children and adults need to learn to think before they act, the retarded people need to even more. If all children need to learn what behavior is appropriate where and when, retarded children need to be told even more explicitly and more often. If adults can benefit from seeing explicit (not pornographic) pictures or films showing intercourse, it will benefit the retarded adult even more. And if all children need to learn respect for themselves and a sense of their own worth, as well as respect for others, retarded children need it even more.

Why do the retarded need these things more than others do?

Most children learn in a combination of ways, from listening, hearing, talking, seeing, sensing — in all the ways we've listed. They are also able to draw both on their own inner resources and other outer informational resources, such as looking for and reading books on their own, seeing movies, talking to others, drawing together the bits and pieces they learn, recognizing subtle nuances, thinking about them and forming them into a general body of knowledge and attitudes. Retarded children learn in the same ways, but they do not have as good ability to comprehend what they're learning and to fit those bits and pieces together. Nor can they draw on outside resources so easily; they require people to help them do so. They will derive thoughts and attitudes, but those thoughts and attitudes will be vague and uncomfortable unless someone helps them sort out and define what they're feeling. They will not develop good judgment unless someone helps them to do so.

You're probably not even aware of how you learned it was inappropriate to hug or kiss strangers, to crawl all over people and stroke them. Possibly nobody even had to tell you that. You just sensed that people got angry or drew back if you got too 'physical' and drew your own conclusions. Retarded children may sense the anger but be unable to figure out the cause. They will only assume that the other person is mad at them, and in their desire to please, will try more hugging and kissing. They need to be told and shown the proper behavior, sometimes over and over again.

You can watch a television program and recognize that it has implications for you or that it's the same thing that you learned another time, in another way. But the retarded person may need help translating facts learned from one situation to another.

I know a two-hundred pound retarded seventeen year old who scared the daylights out of a woman who had been nice to him in a store. His way of thanking her was to stroke her arm, because, as he told us later, "Daddy said ladies like to have their arms stroked." Now he was a lot more impaired than many such people are, but he nearly ended up in jail not because he was incapable of learning or because he had acted upon a wild sex urge, but because his father had forgotten to tell him when ladies like being stroked, and when they don't.

Problems in teaching the retarded.

One of the major problems is that there are so many kinds and levels of impairment that the term 'sex education' itself will be variable. Winifred Kempton gives some very good guidelines for determining what kind of education is appropriate for different levels of retardation. If you have a retarded child, or work with one, you will certainly find her books (listed in the appendix) useful. Briefly, she suggests that sex education be highly individualized, and determined by the student's level of understanding, the reason for the teaching or the goals, and how the material can be most effectively presented.

For example, she suggests that at the lowest level of functioning, a girl may neither comprehend nor need any more information about menstruation than the knowledge that she need not be afraid of it. She may need to actually see the soiled pad of another woman to be assured that it is a natural occurrence. A slightly higher goal might be training to take care of her needs during menstruation, proper behavior, and an attitude of pride in growing up. A moderately retarded young woman could learn about why one menstruates and when. A slightly less retarded person would be interested in and capable of knowing more about reproduction, social relationships and intercourse. The higher educable and borderline level girls would need, want, and be able to use the same information as other young girls.

Some special learning problems.

Categories overlap. One should never assume that because a person has been diagnosed as severely retarded, he or she will not be able to understand or discuss things; nor should one assume that a "borderline" diagnosis means total comprehension. Generally, however, Kempton suggests that the lower the level of intelligence, the more concrete and simple the information should be.

Another problem is that one never can be sure that the person has understood what is being taught. Some children may hear part of a sentence, but blank out for the next part and miss something important without anyone realizing it. Children may look at a picture, think they see it, yet be seeing something different from what the teacher sees. They may say they understand purely out of embarrassment about not understanding. Of course more intelligent people do the same things at times. They're just more likely to realize they've missed something, and to know how to fill in gaps. There's no way to gauge understanding except through continual feedback from others, using every possible way to explain and having the student re-explain. I have seen some schools provide sex education and assume that the retarded are learning along with the other children. Such children often need other approaches which may be only slightly different, yet very important. A fifteen minute television program that is useful for most students, for example, may go much too fast for children who need to stop and think things out slowly; also a typical forty-five minute class may be way too long for their short attention span. Line drawings may be fine for most students, but one of the aspects of "concreteness" is inability to conceptualize. Hence, retarded or brain damaged children may not be able to fill in details with their imagination. If something appears flat on paper, they won't be able to conceptualize the roundness, and need other techniques to help them understand.

Unfortunately there are still too few good audio-visual materials developed for the retarded. Movie and stories simple enough for them to understand are often the basic stories given to three year olds. Yet if a sixteen year old is intellectually three years old, he or she may be faced with problems of a sixteen year old physically and socially, and needs to learn about intercourse and other social behaviors. But, he or she needs such material in terms that a three year old can understand. Until better materials are developed and easily obtainable, teachers and parents will need to use every bit of their creativity.

How do you do this?

You might make up a story, draw pictures, use the door openers created by other needs. For instance, occupational therapists sometimes teach children perceptual skills by having them lie down on a large sheet of paper while someone else traces their body outlines. Then the children fill in the details, learning where the neck is in relation to the head and where the stomach and other parts of their bodies are. If they can do this, they can also learn to fill in the penis or vagina, and breasts. It's the old door opener again. You might try some clay for helping develop a sense of depth about bodies. Clay is easy to work with, allows for easy correction of errors and is fun.

I once had a class of retarded adolescents make clay people while we were talking about sexual characteristics. All we had was red clay, and when it came time to apply the pubic hair, all I could find was some white cotton. Because the students need concrete associations, they weren't satisfied with just a suggestion of hair; they wanted it where ever it went, in abundance, and they weren't too adept at putting it on. With the combination of the red clay and the white cotton, we collected quite an assortment of what appeared to be naked Santa Clauses. I didn't have the courage to let them take their art work home to their parents, but I did show them at a parents' meeting on sex education. The sight of those Santa Clauses was such a marvelous door opener for a group of embarrassed adults that I almost wish I could do it again deliberately.

You will need to focus on appropriate behavior.

Retarded children are often very affectionate and anxious to please. They are extra sensual at times, and like other children, frequently give or receive affection through hugging and caressing. Often adults, because they sense their need for affection, feel sorry for the child, or feel guilty, encourage too much of this behavior. Unfortunately, in effect they are teaching and rewarding behavior which may evenutally lead to trouble. The child needs to learn early and continually that such behavior is only for close relatives or special friends, and that otherwise, hand-shaking is the "adult" way. By the same token, they need to learn that masturbation is private behavior and sexual joking is enjoyed only among close friends. Both Winifred Kempton and Sol Gordon point out that we often allow and encourage behavior in a retarded person that we would not tolerate in anyone else. This is one of the reasons that the retarded often seem to behave in such inappropriate ways.

More emphasis on non-reproductive sexuality.

Reproductive joys of sexuality may need to be toned down, and more emphasis given to the many times and ways that people satisfy sexual needs while planning not to marry or have children. Many will be unable to marry, have children, or even find anyone to date. Adults who give the impression that dating, marrying, or having children is the only good way of life, or who joke about a retarded person's "boyfriend" or "girlfriend," are unintentionally establishing roles their children can not satisfy. Often they do not realize how keenly the retarded feel their difference, or how desperately they want to be like everyone else. Often parents fail to mention birth control until they panic when their children reach adolescence, then see sterilization as the only answer, and wonder why their teenagers are so upset. You can do a lot to forestall such problems by starting early to let the child know that the decision not to have children is made by all kinds of people, for many reasons.

Since the retarded may have limited mobility and a smaller universe from which to draw friends, they may need other options than intercourse even more than other people do. Self-stimulation may be the only outlet available to a few. A homosexual relationship may be more satisfying and helpful than no relationship at all, or a sexual relationship outside of marriage may be the only realistic lifestyle. Again, you can do much to help by thinking ahead. Eventually you may want to consider the possibility of giving them permission for these ways of satisfying their needs.

Problems in denying sexual opportunities.

If you wish your son or daughter to have a heterosexual relationship, you may have to help provide them with both the opportunity and privacy, and if you wish sexual behavior to be private, you must provide opportunity. Too many programs and people try desperately to prevent heterosexual contact. This seldom prevents pregnancies, but it does encourage homosexual behavior and limits heterosexual friendships. It may lead to more pregnancies, since sexual relationships are then furtive and quick, with no time for thinking or planning. Also, while we decry public sexuality, most institutions in the United States (and many parents) provide no opportunity for privacy. In other countries, where retarded adults are seen as having sexual rights, provisions are made even in institutions for people to satisfy their sexual needs in private.

Many parents and teachers worry about exploitation, promiscuity, and unwed pregnancies. It is true retarded children who are anxious to please and who often lack judgment, are often exploited or have intercourse either in a desire to please or because they do not know what is happening. Keeping them uninformed and away from the opposite sex does not decrease such problems— it increases them. The more concrete information they have, the more values, and the more social skills, the more judgment they will use.

You may need to teach social skills more concretely.

Role playing may be more necessary than with more intelligent children, going over the same situations several times. Social skills can be taught in semi-controlled social situations, and we need to do more to provide programs that allow the retarded to engage in social relationships.

Don't deny the handicap.

In an attempt to help the child feel more self-confidence, many people deny the fact of retardation, never mentioning the word. They are the exact opposite of those who never see beyond the handicap. But either extreme is less than helpful. We are all handicapped in some way or another; we need to recognize our limitations, accept them and plan around them, while maintaining self esteem. If a handicap is seen as so terrible that it can't be talked about, that fact in itself undermines self-confidence.

In my sex education class with retarded adolescents, we discussed problems of retardation frequently, using a lot of empathy and humor about how angry one gets when treated like a child and how difficult it is to handle rejection by others. Even though I did not have the same situation, I used many examples from my own life to show that we all suffer from the same feelings at times. We also discussed the ways in which retardation could interfere with judgment, for example—in quickly judging danger from cars or even people; rehearsed potentially dangerous social situations, looked in phone books to find various helping professionals, and made personal directories. We even discussed when it would be helpful to let someone at the other end of the line know they were retarded, and when it wouldn't be. Only two people were upset by this discussion: one was helped by the group and the other needed to discuss his sense of shame about his retardation; the discussion made a good door opener for his own therapist.

All students learned that there was someone in the community ready to help them, learned how to judge when they needed help regarding some situation and how to get that help. That gave them both more self-confidence and better judgment.

Tip:

Many parents note that children or teenagers show no sign of puberty or interest in sex and wonder how they can tell when a child is ready for discussion. The answer is that often they can't. But if they wait for the child to say, "Mother dear, I'm ready to talk about sexual matters now," that child may end up in trouble.

That is why door openers are so useful and need to be used over and over again.

By way of summary, let me give you Sol Gordon's comments that the major information that needs to be imparted can be given in five minutes, although it must be repeated many times and for different levels of understanding: (1) Masturbation is all right; (2) All direct sexual behavior involving the genitals should take place in privacy; (3) Any time a boy and girl who are physically mature have intercourse, they risk pregnancy; (4) Unless both members of a heterosexual couple clearly want to have a baby and understand the responsibilities involved in child rearing, they should use an effective method of birth control; (5) Our society feels that people should not have intercourse until they are about eighteen; (6) Adults should not use children sexually. I suspect he'd add, if asked, that sexual behavior with another person should be only by consent, and that precautions should be taken against venereal disease. Of course he is oversimplifying to dramatize a point. But that really is the essential information. The rest is detailed explanation.

AN ISSUE TO THINK ABOUT

Should all retarded people be sterilized? Or should none?

Underlying this question is the issue of whether retarded persons have the essential sexual rights of all other persons. More and more society has begun to say that they do have these rights, and they should be protected from undue coercion.

Still, even among those professionals who are truly concerned about the rights of retarded children, there is disagreement on the issue of sterilization. Some feel that those with enough impairment to be labeled "retarded" are not capable of raising children to their full potential. Such professionals feel that for both their own and their offsprings' sake, all retarded persons should be prevented from having children. Others consider sterilization or abortion immoral under any circumstances, and point to examples of retarded couples who have successfully raised intelligent children with no adverse effects for either parent or child.

Legally, the situation is indeed difficult, for no matter how fair a parent, doctor or an agency tries to be, one never can be really sure that the retarded person has fully understood what is involved, will not feel coerced, or will not change his or her mind later. My own thinking is that "all's" and "never's" should be avoided for several reasons. There is much we do not yet know about retardation; our ability to diagnose, treat and educate are subject to change. We already know that the retarded vary greatly in their abilities. To merely label a whole group of people as "unfit" is to disregard individual differences and abilities, adopting the kind of thinking that led eventually to the extremes seen in Nazi Germany. Also, there are many of the retarded who know full well that they are incapable of raising children, who do not want children to suffer as they have, and who greatly desire sterilization, yet are denied the same rights as other people in making such a decision. A complicating factor is the fact that some parents will ask for sterilization for their child out of fear; out of guilt for having had a sexual union that resulted in a retarded child, or for other reasons of their own, rather than because of the needs of the child. On the other hand, there are times when a retarded person really is unable to make such a decision, and the parents or guardians are denied their right to act on behalf of that person.

My own opinion is that when the time comes for a final decision concerning the sterilization of a retarded child, it should be made jointly among parents, agency or consulting doctor, a jury of experts on retardation, and to the fullest extent possible, the person him or herself possibly represented by an attorney. All citizens should look carefully at impending legislation, to make sure that in a well-intentioned effort to protect some people's rights, others' rights are not denied.

These are important issues, which the parents need to think about long before their child reaches puberty, for they may affect the whole approach to sex education. Often a geneticist and a counsellor will be helpful in reaching decisions.

Enough of grimness! Joy and humor are as much a part of sex education with retarded people as they are with others. Once freed from the fear of ridicule, they can enjoy a bit of humor, even about themselves, as well as the next person. The following is an example not only of the need to be aware of how unfamiliar words may get interpreted but also of the funny mistakes people make that they, as well as others, can enjoy.

I had been discussing intercourse with my class of retarded adolescents, but the students were filled with tension and fear about the subject. One girl participated from underneath her desk, while one boy had been so embarrassed that he could only listen from outside the room poking his head through an open window every so often to shout, "Hana, hana!" (the Hawaiian "shame, shame!"). The tension was so high that I decided to hold a quick review and end class early. "Who can tell me," I asked, "what sexual intercourse means?" There was a long silence, a cry of "Hana, hana!" from the window, and then one girl bravely raised her hand. Her answer not only broke the tension, but had the class end in roars of laughter. The girl, when informed of her mistake laughed as merrily as everyone else. "I know, I know!" she shouted triumphantly, "Sexual intercourse is when you put the peanuts in the china!"

OTHER PHYSICAL HANDICAPS

In varying degrees, we tend to make the same unrealistic assumptions about others with handicaps that we do with retarded people.   Often we assume that the paraplegic, the spastic or cerebral palsy victim, or the ill or dying have neither sexual needs or abilities.   On the other hand, if a handicap is not visible and doesn't seem to impair mobility, we may not realize that it can hinder both learning and sexual expression and we may fail to give needed help.   Many of the problems and suggestions given for the retarded person will also apply to other handicaps.

The list of handicaps is long: it includes arthritis, cerebral palsy, epilepsy, paraplegia, deafness, blindness, and even after effects of some surgery.   Any given person may suffer from pain, loss of sensation in the genitals or in another area, paralysis, bowel or bladder incontinence, spasticity, inability or difficulty in achieving erections, and many other problems.   Mary Romano, a social worker who has worked extensively with the handicapped, notes that with each of the symptoms, the person and his or her partner, if there is one, will have to individually determine how best to meet sexual and emotional needs within the limitations of the individual disability. But, she points out, in order to know what one wants to do and how to do it, one must know what is physiologically possible. Too often handicapped persons are not given such knowledge.

A parent may feel too uncomfortable to talk about the handicap and may assume that such discussion will build false hopes. A parent or friend may not realize that the person is interested in sex simply because that person is timid about asking questions. Sometimes the parent or another helping person is thinking only of the reproductive aspect of sex, assumes (often incorrectly) that neither conception, childbirth, nor child care is possible, and may rule out other forms of sexual expression such as self-stimulation, manual, oral, or anal stimulation. Sometimes a parent fears that a handicapped child will be sexually exploited, and out of concern, overprotects the child so much from possible rejection that not even the skills necessary for friendship, much less a marital or sexual relationship, are learned. Often the parent, spouse, or helping professionals (doctor, teacher, social worker,) do not know how the handicap affects sexuality.

Spinal cord injury:

We think of spinal injury victims in their wheelchairs, not in sexual relationships. Yet they can and do achieve very good sex lives within the limits of their individual capacities. If impairment is not too great, that can include intercourse, ejaculation and orgasm, conception and childbirth. Even when intercourse is impossible, both the handicapped person and the partner can give and receive sexual pleasure through caressing, oral or anal intercourse and self stimulation. For some people, this may mean changing their ideas about what is acceptable behavior and no one should feel forced to do it. Even when physical orgasm is impossible, the greatest sexual organ of all, the brain, is still intact. Many people unable to have physical orgasms experience gratifying fantasized ones, and when two people are giving each other warmth, affection and intimacy, that is the greatest satisfaction of all.

Spasticity:

The jerky, involuntary movements of diseases like cerebral palsy can certainly interfere with both general and sexual functioning. With aids such as muscle relaxants and attention paid to the times and positions that are most relaxing, not only intercourse, but orgasm can be achieved. Orgasm itself tends to relieve spasticity. Again, the warmth of the relationship is often satisfying enough to make marriage valid even for two very disabled people and intercourse should be neither the goal nor the only route to body pleasure.

Blindness:

The sighted often joke, "Who needs to see what you do in bed? It's the feeling that is such fun!" Having so blithely dismissed the problem, they then completely ignore and isolate the blind, ruling them out not in theory but in practice, as potential dates, marital, or sexual partners.

The blind have the same needs and abilities sexually as other people. They pose special problems in sex education and their blindness imposes social handicaps that indirectly affect their ability to form satisfying social and sexual relationship. Children blind from birth may have difficulty in conceptualizing. Hence they may need special aids to help them learn about gender differences. They may also need help with such basics as adopting attractive facial expressions, how to get on and off buses, or even how to deal with overprotectiveness on the part of a sighted date.

There is too little material available just for the blind. Parents and teachers will need to use the same sort of creative techniques mentioned for the retarded children such as the use of clay, role playing, and the use of dolls and puppets.

Tip:

Anatomical models are often helpful. Often models of the penis are larger than life size and may be frightening to girls or ego deflating to boys. So if you use them, be sure to let the student know how much larger than life the models are.

Deafness:

One of the least noticeable, yet most difficult handicaps to overcome both in sexual expression and in sex education is deafness. While it in no way impairs mobility or sexual ability, it interferes greatly with communication and forming satisfying social or sexual relationships.

Mary Sweeney Smith, an educator in a school for the deaf and the parent of a deaf child, points out that deaf children and adults alike are often kept isolated and lonely. Even when able to form friendships, have dates, and find sexual partners, they are hampered by such mundane problems as being unable to arrange a date by telephone. More basic are the facts that deafness interferes with ability to conceptualize, at least for children who are born deaf, and sign language, while amazingly rich, still has little sexual language.

My husband, giving a lecture to some deaf adults, was talking about sensuality, sexuality, and intimacy. He suddenly began to wonder how such concepts were translated into sign language and learned that they were all given one sign—the sign for intercourse. Hence even useful sex education had become meaningless.

Can you imagine trying to understand a sentence like, "Intercourse is only one part of intercourse; just as important is intercourse, love, intercourse and intercourse." Moreover, the audience, too embarrassed to admit lack of comprehension, had been seemingly enthusiastic and responsive. Had my husband not thought to ask questions, he would never have realized that his remarks were less than helpful.

Despite the problems, experiments in sex education for the deaf have proved most useful. As with other handicaps that impair learning, such courses have used a variety of techniques, including various forms of communication such as speech, lip reading, "signing," and finger spelling, along with visual instruction through slides, film strips, drawing and clay work. Again, parents and teachers can be creative. If you are dealing with such a child, you might use puppets and drama to put across concepts, or make up your own words and gestures. You will need to read books given to the child to make sure that he or she understands the terms used. You might want to learn sign language and even encourage a use of richer sexual symbols.

Some general comments:

When handicapped children and adults are not given adequate information, they still get sex education, but that education is by innuendo that leaves them floundering, uncertain as to what is either acceptable or possible. They suffer from feelings of inadequacy, worthlessness, and unnecessary loneliness, either because they do not realize their full potential, or because they are not helped to deal realistically with those limitations they do have. Sex education can be difficult for both the handicapped and those who act as their educators. It will take creative use of door openers, warmth, empathy, honesty and humor to make it succeed. You can do much by using those qualities and techniques and by helping your children (students or patients) to know that they do have sexual capabilities and can both give and receive love. But perhaps my experience in the school for the blind says it better and will be helpful to those who are apprehensive about tackling such sensitive subjects.

When asked to do a workshop for blind adolescents on very short notice, I was certainly apprehensive. I had little preparation time, knew little about the needs of the blind and had only some hastily gathered props. Also, I was new to Hawaii and some of the students' cultural backgrounds were unknown qualities to me. I only knew some were from those cultures which were 'machismo' oriented and reticent about sexual matters.   Consequently, I stumbled along, often misjudging the amount of sight for each child, approaching some subjects too cautiously and others too aggressively.   Luckily, the students were verbal and enthusiastic and had had a good basic sex education course in public school so that we could cover basic 'plumbing' quickly.

One fifteen year old boy, Tony, was easily the brightest, most socially adept child in the class. No matter how many values we discussed, however, he never got past the dirty joking common at the beginning of any sex education class and any discussion of practical situations ended in his joking about getting a girl into the bedroom. Toward the end, we role played some practical situations. Kim, a usually verbal Korean girl, suddenly became overwhelmed with shyness when asked to role play a casual introduction with Tony. Though he tried valiantly, she finally was excused, in tears, from the exercise. Feeling terrible, I could only provide a bit of empathy during our 'wrap up' and be aware that Tony had suddenly stopped joking and was looking pensive.

The next day, he waited for her before class, and the two walked in late engrossed in conversation with Kim glowing. His next role playing scene during the final class session was with a more verbal girl on a pretend date. They got through beginning amenities, then got stuck. When nobody could offer any other conversational possibilities, I played his (sighted) date. When he again got stuck, I asked about his hobbies, expressing my genuine amazement that he was able to surf and wondering how he managed it. He lit up and talked so long that the class finally burst out laughing, telling him to "Shut up or Mrs. Gochros will get punished for staying out too late." In the wrap up, the girl who had started the role playing scene with him said that she had been so worried about her own acceptability and about the sexual possibilities, she had forgotten to think about Tony's needs. Tony again suddenly turned sober and sat in his seat long after everyone had left.

Finally he said to me, "You know, we got all the facts in school, but the teachers never told us what we really wanted to know, like what went on in screwing or how girls felt. They never talked with me about my blindness. In fact, they never talked with us about anything. I never knew girls were as scared as I was. I never thought about them as human beings, or thought I might have the guts to talk to one about anything except to get her to bed to prove I was as good as anyone else." And then, embarrassed, he rushed off, saying simply, "Thanks!"

That was one of the most meaningful comments I've ever had. It taught me a lot not only about how we treat the handi-capped, but about how we treat all people even in some so-called sex education programs. And it taught me a lot about what all people need in sex education, whether that education is given at school or at home. I'll never forget it!

CHAPTER THIRTEEN

PUTTING NEW IDEAS INTO PRACTICE

We have reached the point where there's not much more to say. But there is a word of general advice.

You may try out some of these ideas and find that they either flop or backfire. DON'T GIVE UP! Let me tell you about social work students (and probably psychiatry and psychology students, too).

They spend a lot of time in 'field work' or in an 'internship,' which means working with just a few people in an agency or clinic, under close supervision, learning how to interview and how to put classroom theory into practice. Many of them have had years of experience before entering graduate school, considered themselves pretty good at interviewing and only came back to school to get a few pointers or to make themselves eligible for promotions. A typical student in this situation, (let's call him John), suddenly feels overwhelmed with new theory and discovers that instead of doing better, he is doing worse. His common sense and intuitive skills fail him, and the more he tries to carry out his supervisor's suggestions, the worse he gets. By the end of the first semester, both he and his supervisor are pretty discouraged, and John is ready to quit school. This period is so common that it is sometimes called the 'November slump,' and in some schools the whole faculty plans in advance for it.

One day in December, the supervisor reads or listens to John doing an interview and it is as if it had been done by someone else. There are mistakes in technique, but it is clear that John is being warm, honest, understanding, full of empathy and communicating beautifully. From that day on, he is no longer a 'student,' but a 'professional,' and needs not supervision, but a little consultation every so often.

What has happened? He looks amazed and says, "I don't know. I just feel more comfortable, but I don't think I'm doing any differently than I ever did." Then he looks a bit sheepish, and apologetically admits that one day he'd gotten so tired and angry about trying to figure out what was 'right,' that he'd said to himself, "Phooey! No matter what I do it's wrong, so I might as well relax, be myself, and do what I darned well feel like doing!"

And that is "what happened." Once he relaxed a bit, the theory had become so much a part of him and his intuition had become so 'educated,' that he was doing the right thing automatically without even thinking about it and even errors were not very important. That will happen with you, too. I wouldn't have written this book if I didn't hope you would try out some of my suggestions. If you quit too soon, they will never work for you any more than they would have for the student, had he quit school in October. But after you've given it some good tries, keep on thinking about these things every so often, relax, and do whatever you "darned well feel like doing." If you're lucky, you'll suddenly wake up some day to realize how automatically and comfortably you have been handling subjects that might once have been very difficult for you. If you're not so lucky, you'll probably be doing it anyhow; you just won't have the satisfaction of realizing it.

As a matter of fact, some people say that their parents never told them anything about sex, and it didn't hurt them a bit. They might be wrong; but it's also possible that those parents did things so automatically and instinctively that they never labeled what they did, and never thought of themselves as giving sex education. If so, that way of doing it is probably the best way of all. But not many people are that instinctively knowledgeable.

Here are some Gochros Pessimist Principles about sex education (or any other part of child rearing) to consider:

1. If there is anything that can go wrong, it probably will.
2. If you have prepared yourself for every conceivable question, your child will either

    a. Ask the one question you never thought of.
    b. Ask the one question you thought of but brushed off because you knew you'd never be able to cope with it.
    c. Never ask any questions at all no matter how many door openers you use.

3. No matter what you do you can't win.
If you are liberal, your child will be either
    a. More radical than you ever meant him to be or
    b. A real 'prude.'
If you are conservative, you child will be either
    a. More prudish than you ever meant him to be, or
    b. A real radical. No matter which way you do it, your child will blame you for any problems he may have, and will deliberately bring his children up differently.

My husband teases me about being a complete pessimist. It's true. But I never let pessimism get in my way! I take my 'Principles' not with one, but about two hundred grains of salt. They let me keep a sense of humor and prevent me from taking myself (or my children) too seriously, so that I can go ahead and do or say what I want without worrying too much.

In the end, I have one more Gochros Principle, which I repeat to myself (in a hopeful voice) about twenty times a day (and believe it or not, I inherited it from my mother, who may have neglected pubic hair, but who had some pretty good ideas on other subjects just as important.) This last principle is: No matter how many mistakes you make, you are probably a very good parent, and your children will probably turn out pretty well, both despite you and because of you.

With that thought in mind, take a minute out to check the appendix and bibliography for tips and resources, close this book, have a cup of coffee, clear your throat, and

ENJOY YOURSELF.

You were already a sex educator before you read this book. Now you are going to become a more helpful one.

APPENDIX

Some sample definitions and explanations that are often difficult for adults to give, especially to young children.

Vagina: Many people just say "A hole between the girl's legs." I prefer the word "opening," so that kids won't visualize a big hole in their bodies. It can be further defined as a little passageway, aisle, or tube that leads to the womb.

Penis: A part of a man or boy's body that hangs down a little way between his legs. It is used for urinating (or whatever word you use with a small child), and for intercourse and making babies. An addition here might be "Sometimes it gets stiff so the man can put it into the woman's vagina. Doing that is called intercourse and is one way a man and woman show their love for each other and the way they make a baby." That is a bit long for a small child, but if appropriate for the age and situation, it's the logical step to take. You might remember that little girls will have difficulty visualizing it. That is why the view of a father or brother or if neither is available, a picture or quick drawing becomes so useful.

Intercourse: The easiest explanation is that a man puts his penis inside the woman's vagina. You may need to also explain that the penis gets stiff or erect so that it can go in. Don't be embarrassed if a child asks how it's done—just say that there are many ways. Often the woman lies down, the man lies on top of her, the woman spreads her legs apart, and either the man or the woman guides the penis into the vagina. Usually people try out lots of ways to see which is the easiest and nicest for them. Chances are your child won't ever think to ask that, but some children do. There's nothing wrong in telling them. If you want to, you can add that children sometimes try to see if they can do it too, but it isn't possible until people are fully grown. Sometimes older girls ask if it hurts. You can explain that the vagina stretches so that it won't hurt except maybe the first few times, when they might be a bit tense. Then the man is extra gentle and can use a lubricant to make the penis slip in and out more easily.

You can tell your daughter to use her own finger to test it out. Too many girls—even women—do not know that this is permissible, or even that they have a vaginal opening. Men can see what they have; it's harder for women. By the time they're in their teens, they should know that it's all right to feel, or even look with the aid of a mirror to see how they are made. How else will they ever know? Also, finger exploration is often necessary to help a teenager learn how to use menstrual tampons.

For young children or retarded adults, you don't need details. Just make a circle with your fingers on one hand, point a finger on the other hand, and put the finger through the circle. You've probably seen that plenty of times as a dirty joke, but there's nothing dirty about it. If you close your fist so that the finger has to work its way into the opening, it shows how the vagina 'gives' to make room. If you keep your little finger clamped shut, it shows that the penis will only go so far, it won't come out the top of her head.

Why do you do it? What does it feel like? Some people say "To make babies." I think that's a bit dishonest. I prefer, "Sometimes to make babies, sometimes to show how much we love each other, and sometimes we do it for fun because it feels good." Menstruation: There are many ways to explain this, and for young children, it usually comes in bits and pieces starting with a one-liner of "It's something that happens to a woman once a month." Many parents and teachers who have to tell the whole story at one sitting expect it to be easy, fail to prepare ahead and discover only after they have cleared their throats and opened their mouths how many potentially frightening words and confusing concepts there are to explain. While trying to find a total explanation for retarded children, I thought one up that would have made life simpler with even my own children. It went like this:

"Our bodies are made so that we can have babies if we want and our bodies are pretty clever. They seem to know when a baby is starting to grow, start storing extra food (actually blood cells) to feed it, and tissue and padding to protect it. Once a month a woman's body gets ready, just in case. Usually we don't want a baby to grow and we prevent it, or sometimes it just doesn't happen. Then the body has all that extra stuff in it that it doesn't need, so the extra stuff dissolves and come out through the vagina. It looks like blood, though it really isn't; we call it menstruation or a period, and wear a special pad to keep it from being so messy."

Of course you fit the words and the amount of detail to the children and the situation. But I found that even retarded children could understand something like that, and it was also a good start on birth control.

Venereal disease: The easiest explanation is "A disease people get if one person who already has the disease has intercourse with another person." I'd avoid saying "A disease you get by having intercourse." You don't want to give the idea that all intercourse produces disease.

Rape: "Forcing someone to have intercourse against his or her will." This is easiest and least frightening if a child already knows what intercourse is. It's unnerving for parents who want to teach that sex is loving, to find that their child's first question is about rape.

Prostitution: If you have explained intercourse early, then it's simple to answer, "Someone who has intercourse for money, (or because someone paid her or him), rather than because he or she loves the person."

Here is a handy answer that will cover a number of questions like, "Why do people kiss, pet, or masturbate?" "Remember we said our bodies were made so that we could have babies if we wanted to? Well, pretend God or Mother Nature made us and then said, 'But what if nobody wants to have babies? What then?' So people were made to feel good when they had intercourse, so that they would want to. But then pretend God thought, 'Well, what if nobody thought about having intercourse in the first place?' So God made our bodies so that it feels good to stroke our skin, and that some parts like the penis and vagina feel especially good. When we cuddle each other, it feels good, and then we think of having intercourse. Even when we don't feel like having intercourse, we still enjoy kissing and caressing and that's part of the way we show affection to each other."

I don't remember exactly why or when I used that, but I do remember that it proved so useful, I decided to save it for future reference. I pass it on to you, maybe it will come in handy some time. You don't have to believe in God to use it—children are good "pretenders" and always enjoy a good story.

Ejaculation: When a man has intercourse, masturbates, or sometimes during a dream at night, his penis gets very stiff, and eventually some thick white fluid comes out. That's called ejaculation, and the fluid is called semen.

Ejaculation is one process that is often difficult for children who have not experienced it to visualize. With this, as well as many other definitions, you may find *The Sex Book* a valuable aid.

BIBLIOGRAPHY

ADULTS

General Books and Articles on Sexuality

Brecher, Ruth, and Brecher, Edward, eds. *An Analysis of Human Sexual Response.* New York: New American Library, 1974.

Masters' and Johnson's famous book explained. Interesting and useful for layman and professional alike.

Ellis, Albert. *The Sensuous Person: Critique and Corrections.* Secaucus, N.J.: Lyle Stuart, 1973.

Albert Ellis is a well known authority on sex and sexual problems and any of his books are worthwhile. This one is considered the most authorative of the popular "sensuous" books.

Gochros, Harvey. "Human Sexuality." *Encyclopedia of Social Work.* 17th ed. New York: National Association of Social Workers, 1977.

Gochros, Harvey, and Gochros, Jean, eds. *The Sexually Oppressed.* New York: Association Press, 1977.

Written for the professional and layman, this anthology of original articles covers many groups who for various reasons have been denied their sexual rights. *See especially:* Leanor Boulin Johnson's "Blacks"; Winifred Kempton's "The Mentally Retarded"; Dennis Ogawa's "The Asian American"; Mary Romano's "The Physically Handicapped"; LeRoy Schultz's "The Sexual Victim"; and Mary Sweeney Smith's "The Deaf."

Gochros, Harvey, and Schultz, Leroy, eds. *Human Sexuality and Social Work*. New York: Association Press, 1972.

Hunt, Morton. *Sexual Behavior in the 1970's*. New York: Playboy Press, 1974.

A Kinsey-like research effort in order to determine changes that have occurred since 1948. Another sample was taken to correct problems in Kinsey's design, although sampling procedures may still be open to question.

Kaplan, Helen Singer. *The New Sex Therapy: Active Treatment of Sexual Dysfunctions*. New York: Brunner-Mazel, 1974.

McCary, James L. *A Complete Sex Education for Parents, Teenagers, and Young Adults*. New York: Van Nostrand Reinhold, 1973.

Written by the author of a widely used textbook on human sexuality, this book may well be your choice for the entire family as your children get older.

————. *Human Sexuality*. New York: D. Van Nostran, 1973.

Mace, David. *The Christian Response to the Sexual Revolution*. Nashville, Tenn.: Abingdon Press, 1970.

David Mace is a well known marriage counsellor.

Masters, William H., and Johnson, Virginia E. *Human Sexual Inadequacy*. Boston: Little, Brown and Co., 1970.

Reuben, David R. *Everything You Always Wanted to Know About Sex and Were Afraid to Ask*. New York: David McKay Co., 1969. See p. 93 for critique.

New Lifestyles

Mazur, Ronald. *The New Intimacy: Open-Ended Marriage and Alternate Life-Styles*. Boston: Beacon Press, 1973.

O'Neill, Nena, and O'Neill, George. *Open Marriage: A New Life Style for Couples.* New York: M. Evans and Co., 1972.

Smith, Bert Kruger. *Insights for Uptights.* Austin Tex.: American Universal Artforms, 1973.

Light, humorous, but useful.

Rape

Brownmiller, Susan. *Against Our Will: Men, Women and Rape.* New York: Simon and Schuster, 1975.

Burgess, Ann W., and Holmstrom, Linda L. *Rape: Victims of Crisis.* Bowie, Md.: Robert J. Brady Co., 1974.

Sexual Variations

Bell, Alan P., and Weisburg, Martin S. *Homosexualities.* New York: Simon and Schuster, 1978.

Clark, Donald. *Loving Someone Gay.* New York: New American Library, 1978.

Provides information and help for anyone concerned about the homosexuality of a son or daughter, friend, relative, or any other loved one.

Miller, Merle. *On Being Different.* New York: Random House, 1971.

A famous journalist tells what it means to be a homosexual and his personal experience in "coming out" when such a declaration was revolutionary.

Pornography

The Report of the Commission on Obscenity and Pornography. New York: Bantam Books, A New York Times Book, 1970.

Sex Education

Gordon, Sol. *Let's Make Sex a Household Word: A Guide for Parents and Teachers*. New York: John Day Co., 1975.

Excellent general discussion, plus information about birth control and venereal disease.

Jackson, Erwin, and Potkay, Charles. "Pre College Influences on Sexual Experiences of Coeds." *The Journal of Sex Research* 9: no. 2 (1973): 143-150.

Johnson, Warren. *Sex Education and Counselling of Special Groups: The Mentally and Physically Handicapped and the Elderly*. Springfield, Ill.: Charles C. Thomas, 1975.

For the professional, but also valuable to the layman.

Kempton, Winifred. *Guidelines for Planning a Training Course on Human Sexuality and the Retarded*. Philadelphia: Planned Parenthood of Southeast Pennsylvania, 1973.

Professionals and parents alike can benefit from both these books.

Kempton, Winifred. *Sex Education for Persons with Disabilities That Hinder Learning: A Teachers Guide*. Scituate, Mass.: Duxbury Press, 1975.

Lewis, Robert. "Parents and Peers: Socialization Agents in the Coital Behavior of Young Adults." *The Journal of Sex Research* 9: no. 2 (1973): 156-171.

Lo Piccolo, Joseph. "Mothers and Daughters: Perceived and Real Differences in Sexual Values." *The Journal of Sex Research* 9: no. 2 (1973): 171-178.

Pomeroy, Wardell B. *Your Child and Sex: A Guide for Parents*. New York: Delacorte Press, 1974.

Rubin, Isadore, and Kirkendall, Lester, eds. *Sex in the Childhood Years*. New York: Association Press, 1970.

————. *Sex in the Adolescent Years*. New York: Association Press, 1968.

Both books are excellent and the authors are well known authorities in their field. Rubin also writes extensively on adult sexuality and Kirkendall, a pioneer in the field of sex education, concerns himself with some of the critical issues we face today.

Schiller, Patricia. *Creative Approach to Sex Education and Counseling*. New York: Association Press, 1973.

For professionals.

Handicapped

De La Cruz, Felix, and La Veck, Gerald D., eds. *Human Sexuality and the Mentally Retarded*. New York: Brunner-Mazel, 1973.

Gordon, Sol. *On Being the Parent of a Handicapped Youth*. New York: New York Association for Brain Injured Children, 1973.

Gordon, Sol. *Sexual Rights for the People . . . Who Happen to be Handicapped*. Syracuse: The Center on Human Policy, 1974.

Hohmann, George. "Considerations in Management of Psychosexual Readjustment in the Cord Injured Male." *Rehabilitation Psychology*. 19: no. 2 (1972): pp. 50-58.

Kempton, Winifred; Bass, Medora; and Gordon, Sol. *Love, Sex and Birth Control for the Mentally Retarded: A Guide for Parents*. Philadelphia: Planned Parenthood of Southeast Pennsylvania, 1971.

A meaty booklet that many parents have found very helpful.

Patullo, Ann. *Puberty in the Girl Who is Retarded*. Arlington, Tex.: National Association for Retarded Children, 1969.

Gives good, practical advice for showing how severely retarded girls can be .educated to take care of themselves during menstruation.

Books for Children

Ages 3-6

Gordon, Sol, and Cohen, Judith. *Did the Sun Shine Before You Were Born: A Sex Education Primer*. New York: The Third Press, 1974.

A beginning book about the family and how it grows.

Gruenberg, Sidonie. *The Wonderful Story of how You were Born*. New York: Doubleday, 1953.

A classic, warm, and nicely illustrated.

Ages 5-11

Gordon, Sol. *Girls are Girls and Boys are Boys: So What's the Difference?* New York: John Day Co., 1974.

Gets into sexual differences, but also tackles sexists attitudes. Non-sexist.

Mayle, Peter. *Where Did I Come From?* Secaucus, N.J.: Lyle Stuart, 1973.

Discusses subjects such as intercourse and orgasm in ways a child can understand. Its humorous illustrations show that people, even parents, need not be young or pretty to be sexual.

Pre-Adolescence Through Young Adulthood

Goldstein, Martin; Haeberle, Erwin; and McBride, Will. *The Sex Book: A Modern Pictorial Encyclopedia.* New York: Seabury Press, 1971.

Most useful for children over ten, its pictures and definitions may be useful to all ages.

Gordon, Sol. *Facts about Sex for Today's Youth.* New York: John Day Co., 1973.

An inexpensive paperback, well illustrated and simple enough to be useful for the mentally retarded teenager.

Pomeroy, Wardell B. *Boys and Sex.* New York: Delacorte Press, 1968.

————. *Girls and Sex.* New York: Delacorte Press, 1969.

Both are excellent books that cover many problems of adolescence. Begins by recommending reading the book for the opposite sex.

OTHER RESOURCES

American Association of Sex Educators and Counsellors
815 15th Street N.W.
Washington, DC 20005

Ed-U. Press
Syracuse University
760 Ostrom Avenue
Syracuse, NY 13210

Sex Information and Education Council of the US (SIECUS)
1855 Broadway
New York, NY 10023
Besides its own literature, it provides extensive resource lists for literature, films and audio-visual aids, both in general sexuality and in specialized areas such as the handicapped.

For information, help, or counselling:
American Association of Sex Educators, Counsellors and Therapists
(AASECT)
44 East 23rd Street
New York, NY 10010
Branches can be found throughout the country and may be listed
as Child and Family Service or Family and Child Service. There
are also Family Service Associations for specific religious groups:
The Catholic Family Service; The Jewish Family Service; and
Lutheran Family Services. All of these will have trained counsel-
lors who will provide help themselves or help you determine the
proper resource for your needs.

Planned Parenthood-World Population
810 Seventh Avenue
New York, NY 10019
Has branches throughout the country and will provide information, literature, medical services, and counselling.

INDEX